Through It All: Wisdom of the Ages

Grace Church International

Seasoned With Grace Seniors Ministry

Atlanta, Georgia, 2014

Through It All: Wisdom of the Ages

An Anthology of Seasoned Wisdom by Grace Church International's Seasoned With Grace Seniors Ministry

DEDICATION

We dedicate this book to all our readers. May each chapter be a beacon for you today and for future generations. We pray that through sharing our stories that you are encouraged to persevere regardless of the challenges that you face. Through it all you can be whatever you want to be and do whatever you want to do when you have faith in God and stay true to yourself. Thank you for sharing in our stories.

Table Of Contents

Through It All: Wisdom of the Ages

Foreword

By: Dr. Toni G. Alvarado

Many of my childhood memories are filled with memories of my grandmother and the elderly people in the church where I grew up on the SouthSide of Chicago. It was the wisdom that I received under their nurture and care that shaped me into the woman, wife, mother and pastor that I am today. I often think of my grandmother who led the Sunday morning devotions with male deacons in our church. I can remember singing my first solo with the senior choir of our church as a young girl and hearing them cheer me on as I began to discover my gift for song and leadership in the local church.

Even as I write this foreword, I am thinking about my Sunday school teachers, Mrs. Bradford and Mrs. Harris, who taught the elementary principles of the Christian faith. I can hear the voices of Deacon Scales and Deacon Fortson as they read the morning scripture, quoting it from memory as if they were actually there when it was written. There was always something special about that little church that made me feel like God was there every week and now I know that much of the peace that I felt in that church came from those elderly men and women who knew God and freely shared about their struggles and relationship with God in such a way that it gave me confidence to trust and know God for myself.

For many years, we prayed that God would draw seasoned saints to our local church. We asked God to send us men and women who had persevered through the storms of life whom we could trust to help us disciple a younger generation in the faith. After several years of us praying this prayer, God began to answer that prayer. One of the first senior persons to join our church was my mother-in-law, Mother Dolores Alvarado. She believed in us so much that she relocated from Columbus, Ohio and resided in Atlanta, Georgia for several years to assist in the work of the Lord at Total Grace Christian Center, now Grace Church International. It was from this place that Mother Alvarado was launched into a full-time career of missionary work in China, yet she deposited in this church a heart for the lost and a hunger to see souls saved in the kingdom of God.

I'm also reminded of another senior gentleman who joined our church in the early years in the person of Brother Charles Barber. He was a retired man who had lived a colorful life and overcome many health and physical challenges and he served in our church during the last years of his life. Brother Barber shared freely of his time, his resources, and most of all he shared freely of his wisdom. He was not an educated man but he was full of wisdom and when he spoke the entire church would listen. In fact, many of the witticisms that he shared during his journey with us are often quoted from our pulpit, like "If I tell you that a monkey dips snuff, you don't have to check his lower lip."

God has been faithful down through the years to send people resources to our local church. One of the most valuable resources that he has sent us are those who have gone through the storm and the rain and have come out singing praises to our heavenly King. The Seasoned with Grace Senior Ministry of Grace Church International is a wealthy field of precious gems. Together, these men and women have compiled years of wisdom into one collection that will encourage and enrich our lives forever. As you read through these stories taken from their life experiences, take in every word and feel every emotion, allowing God to speak to you about His sovereign care and provision. I'm thankful that God placed the seasoned men and women of Grace Church International here for such a time as this, so my children can one day have the same memories of them that I have of those who have gone before me.

Bishop Johnathan E. Alvarado and I personally thank Mrs. K. Nature Mosley-King and Mrs. Mary Moore for having the foresight and wisdom to bring this book project to us. I'm thankful for all those who have unselfishly shared of their struggles to bring comfort to us with the comfort wherein they too have been comforted. Finally, I want to thank God for leaving us with such a rich record of his ability to take us through every storm. I close my thoughts in the words of the hymn writer of old:

"I've had many tears and sorrows, I've had questions of tomorrow, there's been times when I didn't know right from wrong, but in every situation God gave blessed consolation to know that my trials only came to make me strong. I thank Him for the mountains and I thank Him for the valleys, I thank Him for the trials He brought me through, for if I never had a problem, I wouldn't know that God could solve them, I wouldn't know what faith in God could do. Through it all, through it all, I've learned to trust in Jesus, I've learned to trust in God, through it all, through it all, I've learned to depend upon His word."

Read and be blessed...

Dr. Toni G. Alvarado, Co-Pastor

Grace Church International

PREFACE

Through It All: Wisdom Through The Ages give insight into the lives of a group of senior members at Grace Church International. It is filled with words of wisdom that are sure to impact the readers. The seniors hope that each life story will open the way to conscious change, leading to spiritual growth and lessen the impact of some of the hard-knock lessons that life is sure to bring.

As you read this book we pray that you will be greatly refreshed by the obvious mercy of God, new every day. This mercy allows us who have really blown it to repent and make a decision to serve Him wholeheartedly.

A reflection of life, *Through It All: Wisdom Through The Ages*, is a book to treasure and be shared throughout generations. The advice that is written will never be outdated! Through the examples shared you will find encouragement to persevere in trials. God is the same yesterday, today and forever more and if He has done it before, He will do it again! If you are facing adversity we pray that these words will give you a renewed sense of purpose and a quicken awareness of God's plan for your life. May these pages strengthen your faith and love for God so dramatically that your heart is filled with gratitude.

Acknowledgements

First and foremost we give thanks to the Almighty God for blessing us with grace and mercy. Without Him none of our stories could have been told. To Him belong all the glory and honor!

Special thanks to the following people:

- Bishop Johnathan and Dr. Toni Alvarado, Grace Church International Headquarters, who believed in the Seasoned with Grace Senior Ministry and provided valuable advice, feedback and profitable suggestions, and for encouraging us to put our stories on paper. We love and thank you!
- Pastor LaVoris Holloway, Grace Church International at Clayton, for his great heart and unconditional love for the Seasoned with Grace Senior Ministry, and for his constant support and encouragement.
- EbonyJanice for direction, technical support, and for making sure that our stories were published. You were always there to assist us throughout this process.
- Alisha Tatem and Anyango Reggy for lending your eyes to read and edit all our stories. Your skill set has been an asset to us.
- Although our Senior Ambassadors are all young in age, Tanya Dunkin, Lydia Goode, Kimberly King,

Anyango Reggy, Alisha Tatem, and Jem Welch, each one of you has brought so much love and joy to the Seasoned with Grace Ministry. We love you!

- Deacon Steven McNeal, who has been an advocate for the Senior Ministry from day one and who has helped us in every way possible.
- Seasoned with Grace Pre-Seasoned Seniors (ages 49-55) for your continuous support.
- All the Seasoned with Grace Seniors, whether you published a story or not, you were supportive, on the side lines cheering us on! We know that you all have stories and we look forward to your sharing them in the future.
- A special thank you to all those who contributed to the lives and stories of every testimony in this book.

"A SOJOURNER'S TRUTH"

By Jeffrey Lewis

Life, it happens to you. When it happens to you, it affects your entire perspective.

Whether we think we're prepared for it or not, it still happens. Whether we want it or not, it persists. Life will not be ignored. It will not be usurped. Life will not tarry for anyone. It has a divine purpose that it's determined to accomplish. It's determination to objectively usher us along the paths that lead to choices, opportunities, risks and consequences. Sometimes, it sounds almost ominous...haunting...menacing.

Subjectively, life can be seen as a predator, lying wait in the shadows. Sizing up its prey and studying them. Making note of their strengths...but mostly, calculating their weaknesses and their tendencies. And, just as in the animal kingdom, it often seems so unfair that some unaware yet beautiful, vivacious, uniquely crafted creature should fall victim to what the "predator" life does.

And, what does life do?

Life allows countless, even endless opportunities for innumerable possible out-comes. Perhaps, because of where we are in our existence, we have misunderstood just who the actual enemies are. Yes, there are enemies. But life itself is not one of them.

Life, when seen through the right lenses, is our gift from God. It's basically the trans-dimensional vehicle that we're placed in, but we're in the passenger seat rather than the driver's seat. That's hard to accept. God promises us "the ride of our lives" and He delivers, but it's not quite the way we would ever really imagine it. Every human wants to be in complete control of their own destiny. But the truth is, though we do have some influence based on our choices, planning and decision making...we will never have complete control.

Ask Joseph in the Book of Genesis. Who would have thought that just sharing the vision that God gave you with your family could ultimately result in a drastic "tail-spin" that would forever alter the direction of his life, from a favored and beloved son to a cast-a-way, slave, prisoner, and fortune teller. Ultimately, Joseph would meet a great end and become a savior for his estranged family and for the world. But not before he had to negotiate the many unknown and often violent vicissitudes of life.

Do we even need to mention the likes of Moses, David, Esther or Job, just to name a few? Though they may have travelled other "inter-states" or highways of life, they had to struggle to try to maintain a heading or perceived course. I'm sure that historical figures like Abraham Lincoln, Winston Churchill, Ghandi, Mother

Teresa, Martin Luther King, Jr. and Harriet Tubman may want to chime in on this conversation, as well.

Our actual enemies behave much like the predators that I mentioned earlier. They are exacting in their practice of pursuit and punishment. They wait to pounce just beyond the shadows. They lurk on the fringes of our fragile lives, poised to exploit any opportunity to expose our frailties and weaknesses. They patiently stalk and intimidate us. They snarl and howl from the distance, out of our eye sight, trying to redirect our steps. They are intangible, but feel so very apparent.

Where are they? What do they want?

These are the seemingly obvious questions that any human would want to ask. For, if I can see <u>where</u> they are...if I can understand <u>what</u> they want, then I can probably mount a better defense, right?

But, what happens when a defensive posture is not enough? What happens when preparedness falls woefully short? Are "where" and "what" even the best inquiries that could or should muster?

Not "where", not "what?" you say? Then what is the real question?

"Who are we" is the answer that whispered from the shadows and fringes.

Epiphany! Illumination! Revelation!

Yes, yes, that's it! Now I understand. Just knowing *where* they are and *what* they want doesn't expose them. They still linger in the dark. They still track me from just beyond my ability to see them. But...when I finally discover just "who" they are, I can begin to identify them.

Might I say that these enemies are common foes to each of us, every human before us and after us will have to face them at some point in life. They are immortal. They are relentless. They are regard of personal status, means, or pedigree. There are many of these predators, but let me just pull back the covers on a few of the ones that have hunted me. Their names are:

Fear   *Failure*

Frustration   *Hopelessness*

They are mighty hunters of all mankind and of the eternal soul. Their progenitors are sin and death, so they understand just how to stalk, kill, and ultimately destroy their prey. Your enemies may be somewhat different and have different names, but I declare to you that all of our enemies are the offspring of the same parents.

Fear immobilized me. Still does. Fear made me slow my progression towards better and greater opportunities. Fear, at times, halted my ambition and clouded my purpose. It's insidious in its approach. Fear grips like a vice.

Failure sought to drown me. Not much has changed in its tactics. Failure creates a vacuum that robs you of all the rich oxygen needed to even contemplate any kind of success in life. Failure always reminds me of the past. Of all of the yesterdays, it recounts unsuccessful ventures in relationships, education, and career opportunities. Failure has excellent recall. Failure never lets you forget what happened.

Frustration is an agitator. It lives in the present. Frustration continues to show you what's wrong right now. Frustration typically has a very short life span, but while it exists, it's very vocal in its outbursts that state the obvious..."you're still not there" or "how much longer?" Frustration thrives between the start of a thing and the ending of a thing. Frustration is impatient and has no master.

Hopelessness approaches you as a friend. It wears a heavy cloak. It surrounds you at first in an almost comforting way. Hopelessness whispers all of the seemingly apparent things about your situation, like..."it looks real bad" or "it's all over". Then the cloak that it allegedly carried for comfort and protection suddenly becomes a weapon to smother you. Hopelessness is helpful or kind, but rather an usher to the next lower level of misery.

So, where does that leave me?

Truthfully, if they were all I had and all I listened to, then I would have become completely desolate and without hope. I would have been utterly destroyed and cast down.

Failed relationships, disappointing educational endeavors and crazy career changes have seriously complicated my life. Honestly, I've felt (and still do sometimes) seriously swept off course. Failure was something everyone saw me do. It was more public than I wanted. More than once, even when I tried to let go of it, it wouldn't let go of me. It haunted me. Still does sometimes. It's just like a phantom or a vengeful ghost, it pursues me. Blaming others doesn't ward it off for long. Saying that I got a bad rap doesn't change anything. As a matter of fact, nothing changed until I began to own it. At least not in the way you might think, woe is me, I failed! rather saying, "yep, that happened and it hurt and wounded me, but I won't quit."

Disappointment was an irritant. It was present and painful. Analgesics and herbal teas were not going to ease the discomfort. Only the medication of positive change or better-ness would satisfy, but how and when?

Career, really? There are times when I wish that I could have another face-to-face with my high school guidance counselor and share all of my grievances and sure resentments. But, ultimately, those choices and decisions are completely mine.

So, what changed? What's still changing today? My perspective has changed. It's yet evolving and responding. If it wasn't for my walk and faith in Jesus Christ, all of the fears, failures, frustrations and moments of hopelessness would have overwhelmed and consumed me. I've learned not to live a life of comparison, but rather one of commitment, a commitment to better-ness rather than bitterness. Comparison most often sets the welcome mat out for all of the emotions that I've feebly attempted to utilize metaphorically in this literary vignette.

All of our life's enemies would seem to collaborate in a vicious vendetta of human carnage and desolation. It's the Hollywood movie script of the master producer, Satan, to ensure that we never really accomplish all that our Lord intended for us. I'm yet discovering that unless my "dream" is in line with His Dream, then I'm destined for some disappointment and disillusionment. All of that can be avoided when we apply more "acceptance" of His authentic will for our lives.

These words penned were not intended to entertain, but simply express, to be transparent. Life is sometimes complicated, always complex, and seemingly cruel. Yet, it's such a great gift that God gave us! And when we yield ourselves to Him in life's process, we'll reap the best harvests that it has to offer.

Though life is yet transporting me through various challenges, my confidence is that I will not only survive it but actually thrive! So, what do I say to life now? BRING IT ON! I'm always up for a new challenge and you should be too.

"An Impossible Dream"

By Gregory Goode

My story starts in 1965 during my freshman year in high school. I was very excited about being in high school because my two older brothers were already at the same high school. Raised by a single mother with six kids, I wanted to make her proud. Although my counselor's advised against it, I took the college preparatory program in my freshman year. My dream was to finish high school and earn a college degree. Everyone said it was an impossible dream. Although I was smart in school, my mother didn't have the money to send me to college. In spite of that, I was determined I would work hard and earn a college degree.

Throughout my freshman year, I was a quiet student who studied all the time at school and at home. At school I would find a quiet place in the library, in the cafeteria or in the auditorium. Although I attended sports activities and school dances, many of the guys in my classes made jokes about me because I always had my head in the books. As I walked down the halls some of the guys would try to knock my books out of my arms. At this stage of my life, I thought I was grown. I wore a shirt and tie to school every single day. The guys in my class thought I was a nerd. On the other hand, the upper classmen respected me because of my positive attitude. They thought I was older than what I was. I loved it. My two older brothers made the way for me. I walked in their shadow although I was constantly being compared to them. Teachers would make comments like, "You are Maurice's brother" or you are Walter's brother, I am glad you didn't take after them." In actual fact, I set my own standards in high school. I earned good grades and I made the honor roll every six weeks in my freshman year. I was determined to go to college.

In my sophomore year, I again enrolled in the Distributive Education Club of America (DECA) program against my counselor's advice. They thought I couldn't take college preparatory classes. But I showed them! Again I successfully completed all my college preparatory classes and got a job as well. While in DECA, the teacher forced me to take a class on public speaking. Today I really appreciate this teacher because she forced me to break barriers! I ran for President of our local chapter and won. Then I ran for President of our district and I won over the white students from surrounding high schools. The same teacher took me to our Southern Region Conference in Washington, DC, I ran for the Southern Region Vice President over many prejudiced white students. To my surprise, I won again!

My first experience with prejudice was in Birmingham, Alabama. I had taken a flight there by myself during my junior year in high school. This is the first long distance trip without my mother. I was traveling alone. The first night in the hotel I ordered steak for dinner but when I received my food it was terrible. I asked for the manager and I told him my steak was cooked in terrible grease. He apologized and did not charge me for my meal. I did not eat the food that he replaced because I was very upset! I had to pray that night. At this point I had begun to feel like my food was cooked in old grease deliberately because I was black, the establishment was white.

As I continued my high school years, the guys still regarded me as a nerd but I kept making the honor roll. That made me proud and my mother was ecstatic. My senior in high school was interesting. The class pushed me to run for class president against guys that I thought were more popular than me. These guys were sports men. But, to my surprise I was elected class president in 1969. The senior sponsors showed favoritism. Only students whose parents were doctors or well known Pastors in the city or financially well-off were chosen to give graduation speeches. But I graduated with honors. I was in the top ten of my class.

One day recruiters from the University of Notre Dame came to the school searching for black males to become "Fighting Irishmen". I was selected to meet with the recruiters along with a couple of other guys. I was very impressed so I had my counselor to forward my transcript to the school against her will. She didn't think I was what the school was looking for, even though I was an honor student. Well to her surprise (and mine) I got an acceptance letter in the mail with a full academic scholarship. I was excited about going to South Bend, Indiana. My mother, who was a single parent, raising six children, was elated as well. The local newspaper printed an article on my college acceptance. This was major news for my hometown. Everyone was informed about my acceptance to Notre Dame. As I had determined years earlier, I was going to college.

I went to Notre Dame August of 1969. When I arrived at the dormitory, I met my two white roommates. I was the only black guy out of 150 guys who lived in our dormitory, but the fellows accepted me for me. Unfortunately, they introduced me to drinking. We would order a keg of beer every weekend and I drank myself silly. I succumbed to peer-pressure and did what all the rest of the guys were doing. I no longer wanted to be thought of as a nerd.

Due to excessive drinking and partying, I flunked out of college and returned home in 1971. I felt ashamed about flunking out of college. I knew it was nobody's fault but my own. Somehow I overcame the shame. I picked up the pieces of a seemingly broken dream still determined to complete my college education. I enrolled in Tidewater Community College for a year to bring my grades up. I later applied to Temple University in Philadelphia. Through the influence of Bill Cosby, I was accepted with a full scholarship.

Once I got to Philadelphia, I had the black experience. I was no longer the nerd I had been before. I was now a handsome, smooth black joker at a predominately white college. Life rocked! I decided to pierce my ear. I purchased a sleeper for my ear. I attached it on my own and waited until it went through a week later. This piercing enhanced my looks. It caused some people to shy away from me and others to like me more. I was self-conscious about wearing it to church. I would only wear it on week days and weekends.

Philadelphia got me in trouble. I enjoyed the night life all around town. I knew how to ride the subway north, south, east, and west. I was not afraid. My favorite train was the 2:30, north bound train back to campus. I remember one night the train had a car full of laughing people. Someone would crack a joke and we all laughed and laughed.

My epiphany came one night when I came to myself and realized that I was having a good time with newly-found friends, but losing out on my life-long dream. Like the Prodigal Son in Luke chapter 15, I realize my mistakes and decided to get back to where I needed to be. At that point, I got serious with my studies again. I

27

went to all my classes. Even when everyone was out partying or drinking or at the student union building watching television, I was studying. My dream came true in 1975 when I completed my studies and was approved to graduate.

I am grateful that God allowed me to fulfill the dream I had from my youth; to complete my college education. There were some pitfalls on the way, but I got back up, dusted myself off and got back on track. Today I am a teacher, a husband and father, an ordained minister and I have served as a missionary in Ghana and other parts of the world.

"BETTER THAN I DESERVE"

By Vivian McClain

I was born in South Georgia in 1951 in the Red Clay Hills of Early County; a beautiful southern town where love flowed from house to house. The Community and my family loved church and looked forward to attending services on the first and second Sundays at Pleasant Grove and the third and fourth at Shiloh. On one Friday night in October, 1952 it was a beautiful night, cool and black as a pit. The sky was full of stars which lit up the night; you could feel the slight chill in the air. This beautiful night was about to change drastically for me and my family. I was almost 1 years old and I was attending church with my grandmother, whom we affectionately called Doll because she was always all made up with her make-up.

As usual my family was the last to leave church because we were real "talkers" and we just loved people. My uncle Paul yelled to his mom, "Mom are you ready, it is getting late"? My grandmother shouted "I guess so". By the time we were all in the car everyone was gone and the church grounds were empty and dark. My Uncle Arthur tried to start the car but it would not start. This was upsetting to my uncles because they had to push the car to get it to start. The battery was dead and there was no charger. My uncle Art was steering the car and my uncle Paul was pushing it from the back. My auntie Mat says

29

she was there but she was only a kid, so she was no help. My grandmother was holding me in her arms standing on the side of the road praying the car would start soon. Suddenly, we could hear this loud roaring. It was the sound of a car but we could not see the headlights. The car came so quickly toward my family; we only had seconds to react. The drunk driver hit our car and injured my Uncle Art's foot. The rear bumper hit my Uncle Paul as well as sliced my grandmother's stomach. My grandmother yelled, "God help me". She laid there in her blood, clinging for her life. My uncles found a piece of cloth to stop the bleeding. As they were helping my grandmother they realized that I was nowhere to be found. They looked in the dark for me and finally found me when they heard me crying in a ditch.

When we reached the hospital the only injury I sustained was a part of my toenail was missing. No broken bones, no concussion, no snake bite, no head trauma or broken back. That was nothing but God! My grandmother was hospitalized for 6 weeks but everyone else basically walked away with little to no injuries. I believe with all my heart that an Angel caught me that night and placed me in that ditch. Truly God has given me better that I deserve! God had a plan for my life and it was not going to end on a dirt road.

Eighteen years after this eventful night, I started working in Florida with that same Uncle Art, Rev A.C. Lowe, Jr. at Faith Tabernacle Christian Church. I worked very closely with him as souls were being saved, bodies were healed, and people were delivered. I served as a secretary, prison ministry member, choir member, CFO, Clerk, Women Day Organizer and whatever my hands could find to do. My uncle used to tell me, "Sis Niece you were saved from that horrible accident to work here with me". I worked with my uncle in ministry until I moved to Maryland in 1986.

While living in Maryland I attended my 20th High School Class Reunion and it was fabulous. It was good to see old friends and teachers. I was also reunited with a male classmate, Raj. He looked better than he did in high school. He caught the attention of all the ladies. He was very charming and polite. One day as I was talking to my girlfriend I heard this baritone voice saying "Hi, Vivian Marie Foster." I looked around and said, "Hello". That was it. I was in love (so I thought). Raj and I talked the entire weekend. We danced, laughed and had romantic walks in the park. He would look at me and I would stare into his eyes. Before the night was over we kissed and it was great. I felt like a school girl all over again. Raj was smiling after the kiss as if he had kissed Diana Ross. Later in the weekend, I would see him watch me from across the room and my heart would beat fast. He knew just what to do and say and I was eating it all up. He told me he admired me in high school but I was dating an upperclassman so he did not stand a chance.

After the reunion I went back home to Maryland and my co-workers told me I was glowing with joy and they knew the reunion was too much fun and they were right. I came back singing, "I had the time of my life....." Being 40 years old, I began to feel that itch older friends were telling me about. I wanted something new, I wanted something different. And so in 1988 I moved to Atlanta. And coincidently the first place I lived was down the street from Raj. I could not believe this!

The second night I was in town, Raj and I went on a date. We had dinner and Raj gave me a private tour of the city. I started working immediately and enjoyed living in this busy city. Raj and I had long conversations on the phone and dated often but I detected some red flags. The first red flag was Raj was changing jobs too often and his life was not moving as it should. Of course, I thought I could help him. I would suggest that he take some classes and he would take my suggestion as a criticism. He claimed I was controlling and domineering but he would always ask me for money. I was being used and I did not even know. Finally, I learned my lesson and walked away from Raj which was hard to do.

A year had passed and I was doing fine until the day I had to call Raj to talk about business issues. As I was talking to him, I heard a women's voice. Being who I am I asked, "Who is that?" Raj responded, "A friend." I said, "Ok", because it really was not my business and I finished the call and hung up the phone. After the call I started thinking about Raj. That baritone voice sounded so good. Old feelings tried to re-surface. I could not shake him. The days went by and I could not eat nor sleep. I began losing weight. I was a mess. At age 40, I should have known better than to be tripping on some man. But, like my 102 year old grand-dad used to say, "Old rats like cheese too". I think loving the attention of a man is normal whether you are 18 or 81. I thought I was over him but my heart had not healed. I was also embarrassed because I came from a good family with good morals. I could not understand why this man was affecting me like this. After several days, of not eating or sleeping, I called my brother and I told him how my heart had been broken. He prayed for me and said, "Sis I understand and I love you". I also talked with his wife, who ministered to me about how soul ties can be created in a relationship and how they must be broken if I was to move on with my life. She prayed so earnestly for me. I remember feeling God move on my heart that same day. After the call ended I prayed and cried out loud to God. I confessed that I had sinned and made a mess out of my life with someone I should not have been with. From that day God began to restore and heal my heart. Once again, he gave me better than I deserved!

To my sisters and brothers that maybe suffering from a broken heart, emotional hurt, or feel like you are in a ditch on the side of the road, I encourage you to seek God because He heals like no other. Maybe you do not want to tell your story to anyone, it's ok, just go to God in a secret place and I declare He will sweetly heal you and forgive your sins. Sweet Jesus is always there standing just waiting for us to reach out to Him but, most times we come to Him last, yet He still loves us. At the age of 63, I am a witness of God's grace and mercy. I, like the Psalmist know that "The Lord is nigh unto them that are of a broken heart; and saveth such as be of a contrite spirit." Because God has healed my broken heart and saved me, I strive daily to be the "Salt of the Earth". I want to sprinkle and add flavor to everyone I meet, saint or sinner. I don't want my salt to be stuck in the salt shaker. Everyone that crosses my path I want to make a difference in their lives. Someone prayed for me and helped me and I want to pass it on. God has richly blessed me and my family and I know without a doubt it is, "BETTER THAN I DESERVE".

"Broken Chains"
By Zelda B. Lucas

On the second Sunday of July 1958, I was born to teenage parents in Greenville, South Carolina. We moved to Atlanta, Georgia when I was two years old. We traveled back and forth from Georgia to South Carolina because that is where my family was from. My birth mother was fifteen years old and my father was eighteen years old when I was conceived. It was decided that when my parents got pregnant that my birth mother would come to live with my father's parents. When I was six months old my mother decided that she would relocate to New York to better herself, and I would remain with my grandparents who became my mother and father.

On several occasions we went back to South Carolina for funerals. At the age of four, I remember traveling back to Greenville, South Carolina to attend a funeral of a cousin that I did not know. When I viewed the body in the casket, I was so frightened and gripped with fear that I probably looked like the child on the Seven Faces of Eve, which was a movie about a child who was forced to kiss his grandmother in her coffin. When we left South Carolina that next day, the fear did not stay there in Greenville, but it followed me home. I didn't want to be left alone. If Mama moved, I moved. I was scared of the dark and shadows. I was even scared of the cat's hair that would go across my foot. It didn't help that throughout the years my family dibbled and dabbled in witchcraft. They may not have known it, but I learned as I got older what it was. My relatives would sit around and talk about my brother being born with a veil over his face. They believed that a child who was born with a birthing sac over his face had a veil and they could communicate with the spirits. Since my brother had these abilities, my relatives decided they were going to communicate with the dead.

Once I remember my brother writing a letter to his sister who had passed away. He placed the letter under the bed because he was trying to get a number to play. Back then they called the lottery, the bug. Now I am not sure how he was to get the answer, but he and his wife were awakened out of their sleep in the middle of the night with the water running in the bathroom. Now I am assuming that was a sign because he went and looked up the word water in the dream book to play the bug. I don't know if he ever hit, but once again that confirmed that fear in me.

One day we were sitting in Mama's living room and the backdoor kept coming unlocked; they considered that to be a spirit. Once again my brother was sent in to see what the spirit wanted. I didn't care what it wanted. All I knew was my heart was racing because I was scared. My brother thought it was funny. He was laughing so hard. He kept saying, "You ain't scared are you?"

There was another time Mama was standing in the kitchen and she kept seeing a bright light passing in the window, yet again she was trying to figure out what the spirit wanted and again I was scared. This fear took over me for many years. I remember going to my great grandmother's funeral in Honey Path, South Carolina which was in the deep country. Needless to say it was black as night down there. On the day of the funeral we went to a white wooden church sitting on cinder blocks with a cemetery with a lot of twigs around it. The church rocked and reeled when you walked in. I sat in there trembling in my boots. The service got started and I remember my great grandmother's sister danced around the casket until heaven got the news. Now, I didn't know what was going on. I had no idea as a child what she was dancing around the casket for because I had never seen anything like it. One of my great grandmother's sisters jumped up and started taking pictures of her in the casket. Mama almost had a heart attack saying, "Don't let them take no pictures of me in no casket when I die. If they don't take any of me alive then I don't want any laid up in no casket."

My great grandfather came back to live with us after the funeral. We also brought back the funeral flowers and pictures of the deceased relative in the casket. I was already scared; I now had another fear of the deceased person being in the flowers that my grandparents brought back home. I referred to the flowers as the death flowers.

They did not get rid of those flowers because they felt they were a personal memorial; I felt they were demonic and again I was scared. I went to my grandfather's room one night and lo and behold there was that picture of my great grandmother laying there in that casket. I picked up my heart and ran out of there as fast as I could, but the image was still burned in my brain. Mama leaned over and whispered, "They are what you call holiness people". Mama also told me that when she died she did not want to be brought back to "these sticks". She said, "If I wanted to live in these sticks I would still be there". She also said she was just glad to get the heck out of dodge.

Fear continued to grip me throughout the years. I remember as darkness would come over the sky every night, I would be anxious and fear would squeeze me the later it got. I remember lying in the bed, drifting off to sleep and I would be awakened by the bed shaking. I jumped out of the bed and ran into Mama's room. I didn't want to wake her so I just sat in a chair by the bed and stared at her until she woke up. She would look at me and say, "Are you scared?" And I would say, "Yes". Then she would say, "Ok, I'm coming". She would get out of her bed and get in the bed with me and a few seconds later I would be sound asleep. This fear went on for many years, even into adulthood. I married at the age of twenty. One of the reasons that I married so early was because I was determined that I was going to have someone sleep with me every night when the sun went down. I would fall asleep sometimes at night and would have nightmares. I would shake my husband saying, "Wake up, wake up and hug me." He would throw his arms around me and go back to sleep, and I would be laying there trembling until he woke up or until the next morning.

I would still go back to South Carolina with Mama and Daddy sometimes, and I would sit and watch TV all night until the next morning. But I would not stay long because my fear was still associated with that house. I grew up an African Methodist Episcopal church but they never taught us anything about the spirit world. I didn't recognize it then but I recognize it now that the spirit of fear would grip me whenever I was about to try anything new or different. Things like public speaking, going on a job interview, or being called on in the classroom as a child or as an adult made me anxious and scared. The fear caused me to fail many times because I refused to even try for the fear of failure. It was only after I started singing and traveling with Reggie Gay and the Disciples of Christ that I started hearing about how *"God had not given us a spirit of fear but power, love and a sound mind" (2 Timothy 1:7).* The more I continued to hear that scripture, the more I began to examine it and apply it to my own life. I learned that I had the authority over fear through the word of God. So now instead of the devil taunting me, I can crush him and put him under my feet. Stomp the devil out with the blood of Jesus and the power of His word!! I walked in my deliverance and I am still being delivered. I noticed that the spirit of fear tried to attack my two of my sons. My oldest described it as a fear down in his belly, and my middle son tossed and turned at night and was plagued with nightmares. Oh, but I recognized the devil trying to make this thing generational. And that same scripture that delivered me, I spoke over my boys and they walk in victory today as adults without being under the weight of fear. Periodically, fear still continues to come back to grip me, but I am not a baby in the Lord, I am a full grown warrior with the sword of the spirit and ready to behead the devil. I really knew I had been delivered from the fear of death when Mama died. To this day, her body is still the only dead body that I have ever touched.

"GOD DID IT"

By Mary A. Moore

I met my future husband, Bobby, during my sophomore year at O'Bannon High School in Greenville, Mississippi. He was a football player and part-time school janitor. He was a handsome "dude" who I immediately fell for. However, our romance grew during our time at school because my father was very stern and dating at the age of fifteen was out of the question. I played basketball and was allowed to stay after school for practice; this was also a time for the budding romance to grow because Bobby would be around cleaning classrooms. The girl's team was allowed to sit in the bleachers and watch the boys practice; this is where Bobby (and some of the other boys who were around) would join the other girls and me. Although we were always under the watchful eyes of the coaches and other staff, we found a way to pair off and have our "private time" to court, as it was called in those days.

Bobby was scheduled to graduate two years ahead of me and by this time we both had committed to being together for life and he agreed to wait for me. As fate would have it, I completed all required courses and had sufficient credits to graduate after completion of the eleventh grade. My favorite song was, "Some Day We'll Be Together" by Diana Ross and we both felt that my early graduation was confirmation that we were meant to be together! Bobby garnered enough courage to ask my father for my hand in marriage and the rest is history.

After marriage Bobby left Mississippi headed to Detroit, Michigan to look for work while I remained home with my parents. He was a married man and felt that he needed a better career to be able to provide for me and future additions to our family. At that time I thought I wanted seven, yes SEVEN children! He was able to live with an older sister and brother-in-law who helped him look for work. A month later Bobby had found work in a steel mill and was able to pay for my Greyhound bus ticket to Detroit. My first time in Detroit was like being in Hollywood! I was in awe as I traveled from the bus station to the house because there were bright lights, so may cars, and they all seem to be moving at twice the speed that I was accustomed to. I just knew that the taxi driver would kill me before I had a chance to see my husband again!

Shortly after arriving in Detroit, Bobby and I were dealt earth-shattering news when told that his sister and her husband were divorcing and that their house was in foreclosure. We had no other relatives in the city, had made very few friends, had accumulated no money, and felt at a loss. We did not want to return home because this to us would mean failure but we were afraid to get evicted with no place to go. My sister-in-law relocated to Chicago, Illinois, leaving us to fend for ourselves. By the grace of God though our brother-in-law, in his kindness, agreed to let us stay in the house with him until the foreclosure was finalized which gave us ninety days to save money and also find an apartment.

Weeks before foreclosure was finalized we were blessed to move into a one bedroom furnished apartment. Things were looking very good until the other shoe dropped! Bobby was laid-off from his "new" job and I found out that I was pregnant with our first child. Unemployment income of $55.00 bi-weekly was our only income. In addition to rent we had to pay health insurance premiums of $98.00 monthly so that my pregnancy would be covered. Our health insurance coverage through the company terminated after 30 days of no employment. Needless to say, these were some of the roughest, leanest times in our marriage. Jobs were non-existent; all of our friends were being laid-off from their jobs. Welfare (as it was called back then) was **NOT** an option for us. Bobby was a prideful husband. Although we grew up poor in Mississippi, our families never received "free" money and we were not about to start doing so just because we were up North! Neither was writing home asking for money a consideration. So we toughen it out.

I am so thankful for being a part of a large family with little income because growing up we learned how to make money and food stretch. During the recession in our lives, there were many days of eating pinto bean liquor over bread for breakfast, beans for lunch and beans and rice for dinner. Our treat was to have chicken once weekly if the budget allowed this. We washed clothes in the bathtub and hung them around the apartment. There were no telephones, no internet, no cellphones, most days our entertainment was watching TV (there was only one in the apartment) and reading the newspaper, especially the employment section where Bobby marked out places to contact for interviews.

Living in poverty lasted about six months before Bobby found a new job. This was at a steel company with long hours but less pay than what he made at the first job. However, it provided health insurance and the money more than doubled what he was getting in unemployment. Things were looking up!

My pregnancy was not an easy one; I suffered from all-day sickness for the entire nine months. I was so bad that by the sixth month the doctor relented and gave me a prescription that was still in its trial period. He was concerned about possible damage to our baby but the other option was that I would go into early labor and the baby would not survive so we chose to try the pill which worked.

Two months before my delivery date we started looking for a larger apartment. Thank God we did not find one because shortly afterwards Bobby was laid-off from his latest job. This was unexpected and a major blow to our lives. We were faced with having to pay health insurance again and other expenses that were not covered by insurance. In addition to this, we needed things for the baby.

I never imagined my life to be so stressful! I had always dreamed of having a husband, a "knight on a white horse" takes me off in the sunset and I would live like a queen thereafter! After all this is what I was seeing on television! By this time in my life I really need psychological help because I was in deep depression. My husband was not meeting my expectations and there was nothing I could do! It was at this time that I really developed a deep relationship with God. Oh I had known Him and felt close to Him before this but I never felt that I had to totally depend on Him. I thought that I could do it on my own or that I could depend on Bobby to do it. Well, this period in my life, this place where I was, I realized that only God could deliver me, only God could help me. So I did what I had been taught as a child, what I had seen my Father and Mother do, I got down on my knees, big stomach and all, and cried out to God for help. I begged God for forgiveness because I had relegated Him to second place in my life when I knew that He should have been first. I knew that the Bible says in Exodus 20:3, "You shall have no other gods before me" and in 34:14, "Do not worship any other god, for the LORD, whose name is Jealous, is a jealous God". I learned the meaning of these Scriptures as a child so I just needed to put into action what I already knew. Daily I read my Bible, meditated, and prayed and even though my outward circumstances did not change, I gained inner strength. I no longer felt depressed but instead, I had a blessed assurance that God was hearing and that He would answer my prayers. I reflected on the words of my Mother, "He may not come when you want Him to but He is always on time"! I was determined to wait with expectancy because I served a God who could do anything; there was no failure in Him.

Two weeks before our bank account was completely emptied to pay expenses Bobby was called back to the first job at the automobile factory. This was the one that provided great pay and even greater benefits! When he got his first pay check we went looking for a larger apartment again and found one in two days. We realized that God was working in our lives all the time. We did not find this larger apartment earlier because God knew what was coming on Bobby's job and that we would not be able to meet our financial obligations. This time though, He allowed everything to fall in place, even letting us open our first account at the furniture store where we purchased our first living room and bedroom furniture and dinette set. As a bonus, the salesperson threw in a baby bed! Three weeks later that bed was put to use because I gave birth to our first child, a healthy, beautiful baby girl, weighting 7 pounds and 5 ounces. Thank God that the all-day sickness was over!

Our family was moving forward but this time we knew that things would be different because we were putting God first, seeking His Will and being obedient. Forty-four years later Bobby and I are proud parents of a daughter and son, grandparents to two boys and two girls. We relocated from Detroit to Stockbridge, Georgia where we are both retired and living a comfortable life, still trusting in the Lord as Solomon stated in Proverbs 3:5-6

(NIV), "Trust in the LORD with all your heart and lean not on your own understanding; in all your ways submit to him, and he will make your paths straight." We know that this is the Lord's doing and it is marvelous in our eyes (Psalm 118:23)!

"God Don't Like Ugly:
Lessons Learned from My Parents"
By Mae Alice Reggy

In the 1930's my dad migrated from Valdosta, Georgia and found a job under the Works Projects Administration (WPA). This was an economic program passed by Congress in response to the Great Depression. Between 1935 and 1943, the WPA provided almost eight million jobs. During World War II, a defense major plant in northern New Jersey developed weapons and munitions for the military. My mom migrated from Lynchburg, Virginia to stay with her elder sister who worked at the defense plant. My parents met and married in 1939 and settled in northern New Jersey.

My parent's generation found meaning in traditional values and instilled in us the importance of *"keeping our word"*, *"maintaining a good name"*, *"respecting authority"* and so on. Both of our parents were strict disciplinarians. When my brother did wrong, dad whipped him. But my dad never whipped me. He left that to our mom. Every Saturday evening she had one-on-one time with me. She ran water in the bath tub and while scrubbing my back, she would reprimand me for misbehavior. She didn't forget a single one of my misdeeds. *"God don't like ugly"* she'd say. I understood that she was not talking about physical appearance. She was saying that God cares about our behavior and our

49

motives. She talked about values like self-respect and respect for other people. She recited scripture too. *"Trust in the Lord with all your heart and don't rely on what you think you know"* she'd say. Both parents gave me a foundation in the Word of God—and that became my center—my core until this very day.

From the time I was old enough to remember my dad was an ordained minister and served as an unsalaried associate pastor in our small storefront church. For years, he served as church treasurer and handled the church's finances. He also had an itinerant ministry travelling from church to church helping them develop their Sunday schools. I often traveled with him. None of these were paid positions. To support the family, he also worked full-time as a landscaper. He did excellent work. He could turn sand lots into lush gardens with all kinds of plants and flowers. He worked until he died at age 84. My mom started working as a practical nurse, but had to drop out when my brother and I were born. While we were kids, she worked as a maid in the homes of wealthy white families. After we finished school, she joined a home nursing service and continued working until her death at age 72. They passed their work ethic on to me. I started as a volunteer receptionist for the American Red Cross at age 13. I got my first full-time paid job at age 17 and I've been working ever since. They also passed on to me their determination and quest for excellence. Dad used to say: *"A job worth doing is worth doing well."*

Both earned meager salaries, but they were very wise in money matters. They prided themselves on knowing how to live well, but within their means. They didn't believe in buying on credit or putting things on lay-a-way. My mom had a sewing machine and knew how to make clothes. She mended our clothing so we could get more wear out of them. My dad knew how to take second-hand furniture, apply sand paper, a few coats of varnish and make things look brand new. I learned how to handle money from their example. My dad used to boast about that. *"Mae, can stretch a dollar 'til it hollers,"* he'd say. I opened my first savings account at Montclair Savings Bank at age 9 and earned my first dollar at age 17. My dad was so proud that he framed it. In 1944, my parents paid down on a spacious seven-bedroom house in Montclair, New Jersey. They knew how to make ends meet. To cover the mortgage, they rented out rooms. At any given time, four or five families lived with us.

At that time, it was unusual for a low-income African American family to purchase a home in the upper-income part of town. So my parents could not give their actual address to their employers for fear of losing their jobs. During heavy snow storms, mom's employers often insisted on giving her a ride home after a day's work. She had to be dropped off in a low-income part of town and walk home from there so they would not discover where she really lived. Truth be told, I came out of the womb militant. I got involved in the struggle for civil rights as a 7th grade student. I left my school and walked about 2½ miles across town to the rally. I got a whipping that evening because I had no permission to leave school. I am still involved in the struggle for justice and reconciliation. So I wanted my parents to stand up to racism—even quit their jobs if need be. Both of them knew that injustice was wrong, but they never challenged racism and that bothered me. Years later, I remember my mom telling me, *"I didn't get the chance to go beyond third grade. But you will do better than I did."* I understood. By working hard and saving, my parents were able to give my brother and I better opportunities than they had. In their own way, they inspired us to get a good education and challenge injustice.

Growing up in a house full of boarders—none of whom were blood-related—was a lesson in itself. Although the house was large, there was only one bathroom. We also had to share the kitchen. In those days, we had what was known as an icebox. That was a common kitchen appliance before the development of the modern refrigerator. Iceboxes had hollow walls that were lined with tin and packed with cork for insulation. We put a large block of ice near the top of the box and a drip pan underneath to catch water from the melted ice. Every few days, we bought new ice from the iceman who passed through the neighborhood in his truck. Sharing space in the icebox was a challenge. But even when one family's stuff got eaten by mistake, nobody seemed to be angry. Even when everyone was in the kitchen at the same time, no one was quarreling and that impressed me.

Not only did my parents share with the boarders, but they shared their home freely with out-of-town visitors, who needed a meal or a place to stay— at no charge. When I was in high school, four Liberian students appealed to my parents. They were being exploited by another minister who brought them to the USA, then took their passports and forced them to work for more than a year with no pay. My parents allowed them to stay with us. Mom used to say, *"Be careful how you treat strangers, you may be entertaining angels unaware."* My dad liked to go fishing a lot. At times, they kept the fish on ice until they had a hundred or more fish. Then mom cooked and the entire congregation came to our house for a fish fry.

My parents valued people whether they were of higher or lower status. I remember coming home and finding my dad on his knees praying for family members, church members, neighbors and so many others. At that time, I didn't understand why he prayed for the families he worked for or for a neighbor who seemingly out-bid him on a landscaping gig. But he used to say, *"You got to be careful how you treat people. The people you pass on the way up may be the same people you will pass on the way down."*

Until 1954, we had no television. So we had to find fun things to do. Outdoors, we jumped rope or roller skated around the block with neighborhood kids. We could stay outside until the street lights came on. Indoors we played games like checkers or dominoes, or put jigsaw puzzles together. Most evenings we gathered in the living room and listened to the radio—adults and children together. I also liked to read. So I got a library card in first grade. My parents bought story books for me at Christmas time, but I wondered why most of the stories were about white not black children. Even at that early age I decided that I wanted to grow up and write stories about people like me.

My parents loved the Bible. My mind flashes back to seeing my dad putting on his glasses and reading from his thick leather-covered Bible. As I remember, one of my dad's favorite texts was Matthew 25: 12-30. He used to say *"Use wisely what God gives you. If you don't use God-given gifts and opportunities, you will lose them."* From both parents, I learned to love reading and studying the Bible. At that time, my favorite Bible character was Moses. Some people told my mom to whip me when I said things like *"When I grow up, I want to be like Moses —and liberate my people!"* but my mom did not whip me. She knew that God had placed destiny in me and her responsibility was to guide me in the right path.

Montclair was (and still is) a relatively small suburban town with a population of around 38,000. Racism was more hidden than in some of the Southern towns, still *whiteness* remained the standard, and *blackness* remained marginal. Growing up in Montclair, we experienced racial prejudice in one form or another almost every day. I remember relatives being stopped when driving through white neighborhoods. The police just thought the car "looked" stolen. When we entered a department store, the sales ladies watched us. They assumed we would pick up things we had not paid for. We were never allowed to try on dresses or shoes in those stores.

Due to the zoning laws, I attended a predominately white elementary/middle school. Routinely I had to undergo ego-damaging experiences in school. My mind flashes back to the times when a kindergarten teacher made me sit under her desk while the rest of the class sat in chairs and a fifth grade teacher prophesied that *"me and my kind will never be anything"*. I also remember a short, ruddy seventh grade biology teacher who tacked a picture of an ape on the bulletin board and said, *"Negroes descended from apes. Look at her!"* Then he pointed at me.

Montclair had one high school and it was racially mixed, however; teachers (all white except the PE teacher) discouraged African-American students from taking challenging courses. When I wanted to take trigonometry, the teacher told me, "You are a Negro girl. That would be too taxing for you!" When time came round to take college-entrance exams, the teachers pulled the African-American students aside and told us chances are we were not going to make it because most African-American kids don't. It was a self-fulfilling prophecy because towards the end many African-American students gave up. My mind flashes back to a world of school experiences through which I was routinely insulted, humiliated or simply ignored. But I was determined not to allow prejudice to stop me from achieving my goals. From my parents, I learned scriptures that gave me the inner strength to combat racism, classism, sexism and now ageism. *I can do all things through Christ who gives me strength. Philippians 4:13.* For years, I wrote that verse on all my book covers and taped it on the mirrors in the house.

Needless to say, our lives revolved around the church. In those early days, we did not have central heating in the church building. As we lived near the church, it was my dad's responsibility to start the fire in the pot-bellied stove. Rain or shine, he got to church early enough to be sure that the building was well-heated when the congregation arrived. As I remember, my mom's favorite text was Psalms 84:10: *"I had rather be a doorkeeper in the house of my God, than to dwell in the tents of wickedness."* For years she served on the usher board and ushered at our annual convocations. From their example, I learned commitment to serving in the house of God

Nearly every Sunday, one of the auxiliaries cooked dinners to sell and raise money for the church. Most members stayed all day on Sundays for service. We ate together and bonded together like a family. On the week days, I came from school, did homework, ate dinner, and walked to church. In many ways, church was more affirming than school. Most members of our church were working-class people who, like my parents, had migrated from the South. Some were nurses' aides, taxi cab drivers, janitors, garbage collectors, hair dressers, and maids on their jobs, but in the church, they were leaders. On Sundays, deacons lined the front row on one side of the church—all dressed in starched white shirts, dark suits and ties. The mother's board was made up of large-bosomed, gray-haired women dressed in white from head to foot. When they entered the door, ushers rushed to pin corsages on them and lead them to the front row. My dad stood in the pulpit in a black robe with a stole draped over his shoulders.

In those days, we were called *Holy Rollers*—a name used derisively to describe churchgoers who spoke in tongues and '*got happy*' in church. My dad had a deep, masculine voice and although he didn't hoop-and-holler like many other preachers did, people stood up and hollered out *Amen* or *Say that* as he preached. When he reached his high point, some of the saints were swept away in the spirit; ushers were summoned and came waving fans from the local funeral home.

During my childhood, we also had church outside under a huge tent in the summer. Despite street noises, mosquitoes, carbon monoxide-polluted air and August heat, we gathered under the tent. I still remember the smell of sawdust rising in the air as people sang and danced. Vagrants and others sometimes wandered in, causing disruptions. They were prayed for; some left but others got saved and joined our church.

My dad called himself a "read on" preacher. He'd say, "*The Word can preach all by itself.*" In church meetings, he would have me read long passages of biblical text and then he expounded on the text. My mother loved the Lord and every word out of her mouth encouraged us to follow her example. *"You'll go nowhere in life without Christ"* she'd say. She was a preacher too although she rarely got the chance. Although the majority of the church members were women, the headquarters church didn't believe in women preaching. They could speak in the women's meetings, but they couldn't be ordained ministers like the men. So my mom remained in the background cooking dinners, teaching Sunday school, making robes for the choir and helping my dad. Truth be told, I wanted my mom to challenge these man-made traditions. Years later, I remember her telling me, *"In time, you will see things change. Your gifts will make room for you."* Now I understand.

I joined the church choir at age 11. I still remember how the choir at Trinity Temple Church of God in Christ marched in swaying from side to side their voices rising to the ceiling. It was during an August revival meeting that I received Christ. Back then, it was not a simple matter of walking to the front of the church and shaking hands with the pastor. We had to sit on the moaners bench while the church mothers "tarried" over us to be filled with the spirit. The tarry meeting went on for hours. We knelt at the altar, as two or three mothers stood over us repeating the same words over and over.

"Say Jesus," said the one on my left. *"Say it loud like you mean it."*

"Say it faster," said the one on my right as she clapped my hands together

After almost an hour, my head was spinning. I was speaking so fast that I barely knew what I was saying and I fell down on the floor. Then came the release and I was forming words unknown to me.

"She got it," said the church mother.

I got up from the floor with my hands waving in the air. The church members encircled me beating tambourines, clapping and singing.

"Do you know what has happened?" they asked.

"I got the spirit!" I said.

The members continued clapping and dancing round me. Everyone was rejoicing.

There was no baptismal pool in the church building, so we were baptized in the river. I remember my dad standing knee-deep in the water as church members in white robes and shower caps went into the murky water. My mom watched from the sidelines while sharing glasses of freshly-squeezed lemonade and fried chicken with those who had gathered. What precious memories!

Looking back over my life, I can appreciate the rich legacy my parents passed on to me and over the years, I've tried to pass some of these same lessons on to my four daughters. I have tried to set a good example for them and was so happy when each of them accepted Christ in their formative years. I tried to teach them the golden rule, *"To treat others as they want to be treated."* I tried to teach them how to manage resources as well.

When they outgrew their clothes, I taught them to pass them down to the next in line. When their jeans got torn, I designed patches. At first, they objected as normal kids would, but then I told them, *"Just wait. Patches will catch on. You guys are trend setters."* It happened as I said. Soon others were wearing decorative patches as a fashion statement.

While we were living in Kenya, my missionary salary was meager and although their dad had a big job as director of the national academy of sciences, the government routinely froze his salary. My mind flashes back to times when I took them to expensive restaurants and ordered two meals and five plates. At times, it was embarrassing, but I wanted to expose them to this so they would never exchange their virginity for a man's offer of dinner in a restaurant. As my four daughters were raised in a bi-cultural home, I always told them, *"Take the best of your dad's culture and the best of your mom's culture – and be the best 'cause God don't like ugly!"* I am thrilled to see that these same lessons are being taught to my grandchildren. To God be the glory!

Just make sure you stay alert. Keep close watch over yourselves. Don't forget anything of what you've seen. Don't let your heart wander off. Stay vigilant as long as you live. Teach what you've seen and heard to your children and grandchildren. Deuteronomy 4:9 (Message Bible)

"In the Grip of Insanity"
By Robert Williams

The truth is there are strong holds that can strip you of all human values until ultimately you have reached the point where nothing matters. Humiliation means nothing. Living means nothing. Family is either disregarded or abused. Life goes on and you try to re-enter the world around you and regain the person you are, but not before you reach some point in the grip of insanity. The insanity I speak of is not a mental state but a moral dilemma.

My moral dilemma began as a teenager. I wanted to be accepted by my peers and others. So I would do whatever they did, from smoking cigarettes, drinking, and gang fights to drugs. The curiosity of drugs took my life from me. I worked every day putting in numerous hours overtime, just so I could get the amount of drugs I wanted. I was the one boy in the neighborhood that the older folks thought would never get involved in drug activity. I had seen how drugs had destroyed the lives of others around me.

When I reached the point of asking some of the older addicts to shoot me up with a syringe of heroin, they refused. But there was one particular guy I finally convinced to do it for me, after asking him many times. He agreed to do it, but he said he would not be responsible for what happened to me. He asked me, "You see what heroin has done to me and you still want to do it?" I told him yes. I was about to enter a stage of my life that would take years to exit from.

Before long I was doing more and more drugs, even when I told myself I wouldn't. I was doing things I had told myself I would never do, just to get more drugs. Thank God, I never killed anyone.

I reached a point one night when I had spent all the money from my paycheck and had sold all I could from my household. That was not enough; I had to get some more cocaine somehow. Growing up I had watched the super heroes— you know, Ironman, Spiderman, Thor, and Superman. Superman was the one I drew on this night. I knew what I could do, if it would go as planned.

I began walking down the cold, dark street to my destination. I was wearing an army-fatigue jacket and a pair of army boots. My thoughts were racing one after the other, of how I would do what I wanted to do. As I walked at a slower than normal pace, looking down the dark empty street in front of me, I could only hear the bark of the dogs in the nearby yards. As I got closer to the overpass for the expressway, I could hear a few cars whizzing by overhead. The distance to my destination seemed so far away and the night appeared very dreary.

As I walked I also noticed which houses had their porch lights on. One block from my destination I noticed the rust colored fence in front of the condominiums. I was one block away. My heart was beating rapidly as I was trying to form my plan while at the same time looking for any options I might have if things did not go as planned. I decided that I would ask for what I wanted, if the right person appeared at the doorway. Then when he placed it in my hands, I would turn and run for my life. I knew I could always out run in a foot race. My plan would only work if one person came alone outside the pool hall and he would have to be the right person. I knew he would trust putting the package in my hands before I gave him the money.

When I arrived at the pool hall the person I wanted to see emerged from the doorway. I had made plenty of transactions with this guy before and had gained his trust. I told him how much I wanted and he went back inside the paint covered window front pool hall and returned with the package, placing it in my hand. I stood for a moment, then as I removed my hand form my pocket, the thought came; If you are going to do it, now is the time, DO IT!

So I turned and ran. I was only a few feet from the corner. I dashed around the corner heading for the middle of the deserted street. About a half a block down the street I heard the firing of guns behind me, and I could hear the bullets as they hit the parked cars and low brick wall. I started running from side to side, a couple of steps at a time, and ducking trying to avoid being struck by the bullets. As I got close to the first corner bullets were still ringing out in the still of the night. I turned the next corner. My heart was racing fast and I was breathing very heavily. I tried to throw the fatigue jacket off as I continued to run as fast as I could. I had a vision appear to me. It was me lying on the asphalt in the middle of the street dead in a pool of blood.

I slung my jacket back up on my shoulders never slowing my running pace for I knew if I did the vision would be reality. I was very, very, very tired at this point and wanted to stop but knew I could not. I reached the corner and straight ahead of me was the parking lot of the condominium complex, and a fence that I knew had a hole in it large enough for me to fit through without having to slow down too much. Then I noticed that I could no longer hear the gun shots ringing in the night. Where were the people in pursuit of me? I wanted to turn around and look, but felt if I did so it would slow my pace and did not feel safe at the point yet.

` I had reached the point where I had very little stamina or breath, left to run any further. Then I realized that I was near a friend's condominium. As I reached the gate to his yard I pushed the gate open and descended the stairs to his basement area. Then in the echo of the night I heard a female voice say, "Who is that out there?" Before I could catch my breath to answer her, she repeated it again. I told her who I was and she offered me to come inside. While inside I sat still, trying to catch my breath.

She began asking me questions about the gun shots she had heard. When she asked if the shots were being fired at me, I answered in a weak voice yes...not wanting to answer any questions at this time, yet thankful for her allowing me to enter her home. Then she said, "There is blood on the sleeve of your jacket!" I looked and saw blood. So I took the jacket off and to my surprise my arm had a wide and deep gash, deep enough to see my bone. Then as we looked closer we noticed blood on my pants leg, around my inner thigh near my knee. I could not pull my pants off at this time, but I rubbed the area and felt a knot. Never once during my flight did I feel being struck by the bullets, yet I had definitely been shot.

My friend's husband offered to take me to the hospital. I asked him to take me home instead. As we left the house he went ahead of me and opened the car door, then he called to me that it was safe for me to come out. I dashed out the gate and quickly into the car, lying down on the back seat floor area. I was afraid for this guy's safety, because I knew those that I had wronged would not hesitate to do harm to him also, if they saw us together. I did not want anyone else to be harmed because of my misdeeds.

At home I finally felt safe and as if I had achieved a victory, after all my plan had succeeded. Had it really succeeded? I had been shot twice. I thank God for watching over me while I was caught up the in the Grip of Insanity.

Yes, I would like to be able to tell you that my life changed for the better after that night, but it did not. I spent several more years in the Grip of Insanity. I became infected with a deadly disease that doctors and scientist had no cure for, but through God's Grace and Mercy, he healed my body of that disease without me having to take any medications. On my last three appointments, the doctors said they could not understand. They could not detect any disease in my blood. These three appointments covered a period of 18 months (6 months between each appointment).

Today God is my Keeper, God is my Protector, God is my Provider, God is my Healer, and God is my Savior. I understand that I am not here today because of what I did or what I have done, but because of God's Grace and Mercy. Today I stand and serve in church as an usher. Yes me, who was lost, but now I am found. Today I have been ordained a Deacon of the church, yes me, he who was lost, but now I am found. Today I serve in the house of the Lord with Gratitude because I am Grateful that I am no longer caught up in the Grip of Insanity.

"Keeping the Dream Alive"

By Jesse Wright

As I reflect on the recently killings of Michael Brown, Trayvon Martin, and Jordan Davis among others, I can't help but take a walk back in the past to my own experiences with racism in America. I had a real problem deciding what part of my life experiences I would share in this story. Being blessed to reach the rich old age of 69, I have experienced many highs and lows, good and bad times, so I guess in some ways I am a walking history lesson for our younger generation.

In 1959, I was a fifteen year old high school student who was also working a part time job after school in a segregated restaurant downtown on Peachtree Street as a busboy. I would go to school, get out at 3:30 pm, catch a bus to go downtown, report to work by 5:00pm, work until 11:00 pm, get home about 12:30 am, do my homework, and get to bed so I would be ready to get up at 6:00 am to start my daily routine all over again. Let me stop here and give you a glimpse of that bus ride from school to work. There was no Marta; we had trolleys which are street cars that run on electrical tracks overhead. On almost every trip the trolley would jump the electrical track and the driver would have to get out and re-attach the cable that carried the electricity to the engine back on the rail. If this was not bad enough, all trolleys had a six inch white line painted on the floor approximately half way the length of the trolley; this was the dividing line that designated the seating on the bus. All seats in front of the white line were designated for white passengers, the seats behind the white line were for Negro riders (Negros were considered to be riders not passengers). If the white section filled up in front of the white line they would move behind the white line and the Negro riders were required to move further back to the rear. If the Negro section filled up and there were still seats in the white section, Negros we required to stand no matter how many empty seats were vacant in front of the white line.

In addition, there were very few public restrooms or water fountains downtown for Negro patrons, and no restaurants or movie theaters. Negroes were served out of the back doors of food establishments. If you had the courage to go to the movies you sat in the balcony. During that time, young black men were harassed by the police similar to what we are seeing today (It seems like some things just don't change). I remember the first black police officer that was hired by the city of Atlanta, his name was Strickland. He had no arrest powers over white citizens. If he observed a white person doing something against the law he would have to call it in and follow the person until a white officer responded and made the arrest if they chose to do so. Because I worked at night I was a constant target of harassment by the police. The trolley would stop running so I was forced to walk home.

As I mentioned earlier, I worked for a restaurant downtown, one of the patrons that frequented that establishment was a member of the Georgia state board of pardon and parole. His name was Judge J.W. Claxton. Over time I got to know the judge by assisting his wait person when he was in the restaurant. He took a personal interest in me after a while and whenever he would come in he would have me come out to his private dining area and we would talk. He would inquire about my family and how I was managing to work and go to school. He was really concerned that I would drop out of school before I graduated. During one of these conversations, I told him about the problem I was having walking home at night and the harassment I was getting from the police. He told me he would take care of that, and the next time he came in he had a letter and one of his cards attached to it. He instructed me to carry that letter at all times when I was out and if I had any problems with anyone I was to get in touch with him day or night. The letter instructed whom it concerned that I was to be allowed to proceed any time day or night without hesitation and harassment. This didn't completely solve my problem, but it did help. Judge Claxton was one of those white people that made things happen behind the scene. There were others that used their influence to help but most of this was done behind the scenes because of the ridicule they would have endured if their actions and help were made public.

In 1964 when President Lyndon Johnson signed the Civil Rights Bill ending segregation in all public facilities, the owners of Seven Steers restaurants ordered the managers of all seven restaurants to immediately integrate all facilities by opening the doors to all patrons, and to start elevating the Negro staff into responsible and management positions. I was put in a manager trainee position per the request of Judge J.W. Claxton. Judge Claxton and I remained friends until his death in 1987. Through his support, both financial and moral, I was able to complete high school, and I went on to be the first black manager of the Seven Steers restaurant that once stood in the empty space next door to the Georgian Terrace hotel on Peachtree street across from the famous Fox Theater. This is where I was 54 years ago and what Atlanta was like then.

After working for about five additional years for the restaurant chain, I decided that I wanted to leave Georgia and see some of the world. I wanted to see if people in other parts of the country and the world had the same racist mentality that I had experienced all my life in Georgia. In 1968, I joined the United States Air Force and was assigned to the Security Police Division. My first assignment was Kansan, Korea. It surprised me that racism existed among U.S. military fighting men. When you have to depend on each other to stay alive, there is still time to hate. There were incidents of white airman assaulting other white airman for associating with black airman (Note we had moved from being Negro to black). There were four white guys that I went through basic training and police training school with that were also sent to Korea at the same time as I was. We became friends and spent a lot of time together when we were not on duty. We all were subjected to ridicule by both white and black airman. We didn't allow this to break the bond we had formed. After 13 months we were sent back to the United States and all sent to different locations, however, we all kept in touch over the years and remained friends the whole time we were in service.

During my time in service, I was stationed in Maine, North Dakota, Colorado, Texas, Vietnam, and Spain. Of all the assignments that I had, Spain was the one place where the local population accepted everyone for who they were and not by the complexion of their skin. When I got out the service, I gave serious thought to moving to Madrid and becoming a full time resident. However, no matter how bad things might be, there is no place like home.

I got out of the service in 1981 and returned to Colorado Springs to live. I noticed a big change in race relations over the years, but the reality is that no matter where you go in the good old USA we still had a major problem with whites accepting blacks as equals and some blacks accepting being treated as an equal. Old habits are hard to break on both sides. This is still as true today as it was in 1963 before the Civil Rights Bill was passed.

Maybe seeing what has happened in the past two years with young black men being killed without the perpetrators being punished for their deeds will be a wakeup call for all people in this nation. Over the years we have lost too many of our young people to violence from the police, gangs, accidental killings, and let's not forget the prison system that is taking our young men and women at a rate of 3 to 1 over any other population. This is very troubling to me and should be for every person in America no matter your race. The United States is the only country in the free world that identifies its citizens by race or the color of one's skin. Every American citizen has an obligation to speak up and speak out against the violation of the rights of all citizens based on their color, creed, gender, personal preferences, or socioeconomic status. As Dr. Martin King Jr. once said, "Injustice anywhere is a threat to justice everywhere".

I must admit there was a time when I was very anti-white; I saw every white person as the one that had tried to make me feel like an outsider in this country that was built on the backs and with the blood and sweat of my ancestors. At times this anger and hatred was so intense I would look for ways to invoke confrontation with any white person I encountered. After years of carrying this anger and hatred, I finally realized that I was just as guilty of being a racist as the people I had hated for all those years. I took my situation to God in prayer and he assured me that he would cleanse my heart of the hurt, anger, and deep seated resentment that I carried. I gave over my heart, mind, and soul to Christ and asked for forgiveness for all the hurt and pain I had afflicted on people whom had no responsibility for what others were doing.

In 1975, I was called into the ministry to work and take God's word to all that was weary and heavy laden in need of a sweet resting place. I stood on the front lines for many years. I went through some very difficult times in my life and felt that I was not worthy to continue to lead as a pastor. I stepped aside from my pastoral duties, but I never stepped aside from God and the church. I miss my pastoral duties, but I feel I have received a calling that is just as important. This is where I've been. This has been a long hard journey, but I'm no way tired.

On February 15, 2007, I was hired by Total Grace Christian Center. After being a part of this church for a few months, I noticed something was happening that I couldn't really explain. On Sunday mornings I would stand in the corridor to be available if someone needed assistance or help. As people got to know me and expected to see me in the corridor on Sunday mornings, some of the young men and women would come up to me to share with me their experiences in school, about their involvement at the church, and whatever else was on their mind. They would ask my advice and seek my approval. As they would advance in school and finally reach the point of graduation, I would receive invitations to attend.

Some who joined the military would often times update me on how things were going and reflect on earlier conversations I had had with them, this was sometimes what nudged them to move forward. I still receive letters from some of these young people who are making their mark in service and college. Some of these young people have told me that even though I am an older person they feel comfortable being able to talk about what is on their minds without fear of being ridiculed or looked down on.

Based on my interactions with young people here are some of my observations:

- Our young people are our future, we have to love and appreciate them, protect them with our very lives. We as parents and grandparents have an obligation to our youth to counsel, advice, lead, and above all else set an example that they can follow.

- In order to demand respect from others, we must teach our young men to pull up their pants and our young ladies to act and dress like ladies.

- We must remind our young men that they are judged by what comes out of their mouths, so they have to stop using language that they wouldn't use in front of their mothers or sisters.

- When a young person does something that you disapprove of, instead of getting angry and yelling, explain why this behavior is unacceptable. Sometimes we must bend a little so we don't break their spirits and lose them.

- As a parent, I did my best to teach my children values and how to survive in a society that is far from ideal. I make an effort to see my grandkids as regularly as possible, to assure them that they know and understand love as well as discipline; this is a very important part of them growing up to be productive citizens. When we as parents and grandparents come to realize that we have an obligation to be role models and mentors rather than trying to be best friends with our young people, will we see the changes that are much needed in our community.

- Every man and women has an obligation to our youth, you don't have to be a birth parent to be a role model and mentor. Don't be selfish; share your knowledge and experiences with our young people.

- Correct when it's needed and praise when it's deserved.

I have taken a long hard look over the past 69 years of my life and have

come to realize that we have made some progress in this country but there is much work to be done. With the signing of the Voting Rights Act, African Americans were given the right to cast our ballots to help shape the direction of this nation. However, voter turnout among blacks is lower today than it was in 1964; our high school dropout rates have skyrocketed in recent years; the murder rate of blacks by blacks by, both older and young men, has reached epidemic proportions; and the murder rate of blacks by white perpetrators is on the increase and the tragic facts are they are going unpunished. So we must ask ourselves, with all the progress that has been made over the past 50 or 60 years, how much better off are we today than we were then? We have earned our civil rights yet we fail to exercise them. Business as usual is not acceptable anymore.

I pray that God will see fit in his divine wisdom to allow me to witness a turnaround in the way we deal with the problems our young people are facing each day. I am looking forward to the day when our young men greet each other with a handshake instead of a 357 magnum; when our young ladies concentrate on being the best they can be instead of trying to be the most popular with the boys; and I want to see substantial reforms in the criminal justice system. I plan on dedicating more time and energy toward helping our young people get prepared to take over and lead this nation and our race to a more stable and rewarding future. I challenge each of you to take a young person and become a mentor, spend time with them, and show them that we all care about where they are and where they are headed. Remember, they are our future and without a future we can only revert to the past and believe me we don't want to go backward. With your caring and nurturing we can turn this around and look forward to a much brighter and prosperous future and we make it happen by caring for our next generation of men and women. I pray for wisdom and guidance each day so I can pass it on to someone that will make a difference to our future. I ask you to help fulfill this old man's dreams.

"Let the Redeemed of the Lord Say So"

By Eunice Heath

Yes I can say so! I know I have been redeemed and anybody that knew me back then, can say --- so too! I am one of the ones that survived the trials and tribulations of a spoiled brat youth growing up in the suburbs of New York. Oh, don't get me wrong now, I had a wonderful childhood. I came from a very loving and caring, mid-income, homeowners, Cadillac driving, entrepreneurial family. I had a mother and a father together in the same house. My father was the ideal father that loved his family, took care of his family, and made sure we had food on the table and a roof over our heads. He also made sure that there was a plenty of Johnny Walker Red and Heinekens in the refrigerator. Had an older brother twenty years my senior who was in the Air Force overseas with his wife and three kids. My father made sure that he was going to be there because he told me the story of how he wished he had a father so many times when he was a young boy. You see, my father was the youngest of four children. He was the youngest of three boys and one girl who is next to him in age.

My grandmother Eunice, whom I am named after, died giving birth to him in Stone Mountain, Georgia. My father, James, never knew his mother. His father left soon

79

after to go north to Detroit, Michigan where the jobs were more plentiful, because back in that time, that was what the men of the South did. He couldn't raise "four children with no wife" is what I'm told he said and soon after the birth of my father and the death of his wife, that's what he did. Now he was good with sending money and clothes back for his children and to their grandmother, Clara, to help raise his children, but he never came back home.....alive that is. As the story goes, Clara wasn't all that pleased to have to start raising four little snot nosed kids after raising her own nine or ten children, so the kids were split up after they got a little bigger. The eldest, was soon old enough to go off to the army, the next oldest son, was shipped down to Union Point to an uncle to help with his fields, and the little girl was also sent for a while to somebody but was soon returned to help great grandmother Clara and great grandfather Early as they were getting up in age. It is said that Clara had started losing her mind and on one hot sunny July day decided to go to town in her fur coat that my grandfather had sent to her from Detroit where it snows a lot. They knew something wasn't quite right with Clara then. But back to the part of why my father told me that he wanted me to know that he would never leave me as I was his beautiful and only daughter and he knew what it was like to not have a father. Much like my Heavenly Father who has let me know that He has redeemed me and will never leave me nor forsake me.

My mother, Mary, was the ideal Southern Belle being born the eldest of   fourteen children in North Carolina. She knew how to cook anything! And anything she cooked tasted wonderful. I can truly say that I really appreciated her cooking so much more when I was living out in California eating Lays potato chips for breakfast, lunch, and dinner when my so-called grown self-decided to leave the comforts of my loving family and go out to the West Coast to be with my first fiancé who was in the Navy stationed in San Diego, California. Eventually, he got locked up at the tender age of nineteen or twenty. I was so young, yet so much in love.

I thought I knew everything. Boy was I ever so glad when my Mama heard it in my voice that everything wasn't alright and she told me to get my you know what to that you know what airport and get on that you know what airplane. "But Ma, I don't have any more money" and she said in her most loving sweet angelic voice, "I will have a ticket waiting for you." Now whether you know it or not, a mother is Super Woman in disguise. If you didn't know it, let me tell you, they all are. Thank God she made me finish college.

Ok, so now you can understand that for a long time I could be that person that stands on top of Stone Mountain and shouts "SO!" because there have been so many times that I have been redeemed. I was redeemed from my own destruction of myself. So when I got back on the East Coast, no man was safe. Have you ever heard that hurting people...hurt people? I used to have this guy friend who was my cocaine connection. He served two purposes in life me. Yep, you guessed it, sex and he supplied me with drugs. Now I was not the ultimate user, oh no, I was about the Benjamin's (money). I loved to party and loved to look good, so main purpose was to make sure that happened. For some reason he began to think that he was the only person in my life. I happened to be hanging out with him in Connecticut on one of those drug pickups and drop offs when I left with my package to go out to the clubs in New York. I had just crossed the Mianus Bridge on interstate 95 before the bridge collapsed. Trucks and cars tumbled into the water right there at Old Greenwich. We didn't have cell phones at that time and I just couldn't understand why my mom and dad were waiting for me at the door the next morning when I finally did get home so happy and glad to see me. You see, my lover had heard about the bridge collapsing and many people getting killed. He called my mom and dad very early and was crying and saying, "I'm sorry, I'm so so sorry. Eunice and I were hanging out and I tried to get her to spend the night and she insisted on going to the city to party and I'm sorry." I don't know what all he said, but when I returned I received so much love. They all thought I was at the bottom of the Mianus Bridge in the river.

After that incident, I didn't bother with my lover much more. I kind of knew I was playing with fire; he thought he was supposed to look after me or something. I don't know, maybe it was my "inner man" (my soul) telling me back then but something steered me in a different direction.

I thank God for great parents who had me late in life and who knew some things about life because I thought I knew it all growing up in New York. My mother was like a sweet and sour candy – you knew you had candy but you also had the reminder of how bitter it could be if you tried her. You see I thought my mom couldn't run one day and I tried her, she made me mad and I said something under my breath that I just knew she didn't hear and when she started coming for me, I took off running, thinking surely my young energetic legs could out run this old woman. Baby, when I woke up, I realized I wouldn't try that ever in life again. You do not curse an African American mom that happens to be the source of life for you. Oh yeah, I forgot to tell you I was a little spoiled growing up, but they knew just when to let me know that they were still in control. Nothing like parents today! But I would rather have had the rod of correction than the Correction Facility. Like the one time I wanted these cute little Cinderella high heels that were in the toy department at Kings Department Store – sort of like the WalMart of that area in Stamford, Connecticut. I probably was about three or four years old at the time. Well my mother ,unbeknown to me, was getting those cute little Cinderella high heeled shoes for me for Christmas or my birthday, but I wanted them right then and there. She said," No put those shoes back, we'll let Santa Claus bring them to you if you will be good." Of course that defiant side of me was not thinking about Santa Claus, the Easter Bunny, or no one else, I wanted those shoes! Period! Well, again my mother said, "put the shoes back." I wasn't having it. I had made up in my mind that they were going home with me that day, that moment. The tug of war started but I lost the battle. I do remember being on the floor of King's Department Store having a temper tantrum. The next thing I remember is being outside the store where these little bushes were with these things on them called switches. Needless to say, I had a talk back spirit too for a little person for a short time in my life too, and when I said, "I'm gonna tell my daddy", all I remember her saying is, "I'll whip your daddy's butt too!" I cried all the way home and when I got home, I cried all the way to sleep. I didn't get those cute little Cinderella high heeled shoes until Christmas and by that time, I didn't even want them. But I can say that I never had to have a conference at King's Department Store ever again. Yep, I was good.

Now let me tell you that life has been sweet to me but I have had my share of heartaches. For instance, the time I caught my boyfriend cheating on me.... this was just after I had buried my mother. Not only did I sic my Doberman Pinscher dog on him, , but I took my pink pearled handle twenty-two pistol that my uncle John had given me and shot at him. The dog got confused with the loud sound of the shot and that's the only reason that boyfriend is alive. It wasn't so much about him cheating on me, but that he had the audacity to lie to me. When I wrapped that dog chain around my fist and was swinging at him and broke his fifty gallon fish tank and all his exotic fish came pouring out, he punched me! He pushed me back into the glass top table and I fell through it and cut my butt ! He called my dad and told him that I tried to kill him. That was the second time I had ever seen my daddy cry; once at my mamma's funeral and when he was on bended knee with me when I finally got home pleading with me to please give him the gun and he couldn't stand the thought of me being in jail or dead. I didn't even know my butt was cut. I didn't want to give up my pink pearl handled twenty-two pistol, but I did. I cried because my daddy was crying and because he loved me. My daddy was praying and crying and I realized I didn't want him to have to bury me so soon after burying my mom. I had to take care of my daddy. My boyfriend moved out of state. I had promised him I was going to kill him - it was not a threat but a promise.

But you really want to know how I know that I have been redeemed? There have been many trials and tribulations but the one that changed my life is when I was burning the candle at both ends while living alone in Georgia. My sweet saved cousins had been asking me to come go to church with them time and time again but, I hadn't taken them up on the offer yet because, see I was red hot and rolling – had a candy apple red Corvette, my own three story four side brick house, and was doing a lot of things, some good and some not. Oh, mamma didn't raise no fool now. A whole lot of changes had gone down between birth in Detroit, to being raised in Stamford, Connecticut and Mt. Vernon, New York, to living in Oceanside, California, East Orange, New Jersey, and Tobyhanna, Pennsylvania. I have been in situations that as the old people say, "it was a knat's rear end that I got away", doing things I knew I shouldn't have been doing – illegally and thinking I'm bigger than my 5' self. Shucks, the gun I was carrying was almost larger than I was but thank God for mamma's prayers. Thank God for not letting me die out in my mess. I thank God for bringing me back from a severe case of Bell's Palsy where I couldn't even talk or raise my right arm.

You see, in 1991 I moved to Big Canoe, Georgia with yet another fiancé. We had it going on for about two years--- but then things feel apart. I called the North American Moving Van lines and asked them if they could empty a three story house in the mountains overlooking the mountains and the lakes and all that in six hours because the only thing I was going to leave in that house was a body. Well they said yes and I gave them the date and the time. Now as God would have it, He didn't want me spending the rest of my days in jail. He conveniently did not let that soon-to-be-dead-person come home that night. So I moved without any problems. I moved everything into a storage unit and I vowed to not have to pay for the second month because the first month was only $1.00. Between Thanksgiving and Christmas, I commissioned five realtors to look for me a house and you know they all want you to work with them exclusively but I was a woman on a mission. I had never lived in an apartment and I was determined that I wasn't going to let no man be the cause of me living in an apartment now, thank you very much. I found a house that spoke to me the moment I walked in. Not only did the house speak to me, but the realtor had to leave the house key on the electric box because someone had broken a key off in the realtor's box so they couldn't put the key in the box. Why did she tell me that? After we were done and said our kudos, I went straight away back to the house and told the house that it was mine and walked around it seven times (like the walls of Jericho), put the key on my key ring and kept on moving. How about no one else wanted to see the house, no one inquired about the key and the house was owned by the bank so there wasn't anyone to bicker with. Everything went smoothly at the closing which happened right after my birthday in January. The realtor said, "I have never had a closing go this smoothly and where they gave you everything you asked and assistance money too…" At that time there were several programs to help like "First Time Buyer", "African American Woman Buyer", "A Whatever You Want Buyer". Hey she didn't know who I knew…..

At this point, I now had my home, and my own two cars in the garage . I was not thinking about being consistent with my walk with the Lord. I knew of Him. My mother's father built their church from the ground up so I knew how to do the African Methodist Episcopal walk. My father's family church was established with my great grandparents so I knew how to do the Union Missionary Baptist walk. But it was when my Pentecostal cousins finally got me to go to church with them after I was struck with Bell's Palsy and when I couldn't do for myself that I started to have a relationship with the Lord. When I look back at how God had protected me and kept me through many dangers, I can only say --- thank you!

When that one Wednesday night came, I had been out of the hospital and only a short time had passed when the doctors had said that only twenty percent of people with this severe case come out of it. It was then that I realized that God had a purpose for my life and it wasn't to be a fool doing the foolish things I was doing. On that August Wednesday night at the mid-week service, I went to church with my cousins. The Superintendent of the Eastern District of the COGIC churches was leading Bible Study. He would have everyone read a few verses of the chapter they were studying. It was at that service that I began to put things together in my mind. You see Bell's Palsy affects your mind. It is a neurological interruption. I would be thinking things but would not be able to speak what I was thinking, similar to a stroke victim. My cousins had come to pick me up; I was so un-organized in my mind that I couldn't even put my clothes and shoes on right. This was not me. Not the fashion plate from New York who had to wear the latest and greatest fashions right off of Fifth Avenue.

When I got to the church, I saw these beautiful people reading from the Bible. I thought "Man, I want to do that! I want to read something from the Bible." Now, my face was severely twisted. My left eye would not close at all. My mouth drooled. My words were not audible. But I wanted to read from the Bible like those people were doing. I jumped up to read and my eyes could not focus but I started reading. The members of the congregations started looking at me and coming over to me and shouting and crying and screaming. I --- wondered what their problem was, "I'm just reading like I saw them do". Lo and behold they were witnessing a miracle! You see, they knew my story before I got there. My cousins had been praying for me. They had asked the church to pray for me. They told me that they knew a Man who could heal me. I thought they were talking about the pastor and from my recollection, I had not seen that happen before. But on that August Wednesday night at mid-week Bible Study, I was redeemed from the enemy's hand of a disoriented mind, a life of destruction, and a life of hurt. The church went into praise and worship. The congregants were hugging me and touching me and I just kept on reading. As it was told, at first they didn't understand a word I was saying, but then, they said my face starting shifting and my words got clearer and clearer. My eyes started looking normal and my words were words that were of the Lord. I was looking at the Bible but what verse and chapter I do not know. I was just reading the Bible like I saw those beautiful people doing.

I knew I had been redeemed. I can say "SO"

"Let the redeemed of the Lord say so, whom he hath redeemed from the hand of the enemy" (Psalms 107:2)

"MEETING AND OVERCOMING CHALLENGES"

By Margaret Griffin Baker

As we go through this journey called life we all encounter some adversities or challenges. The outcome depends on how we look at them and how we handle them. I chose to look at them as "life" challenges that can be dealt with and overcome. As I reflect back on my life I thank God for keeping me during those times.

The most defining moment of my life happened on August 15, 1968. I was getting dressed when I heard my mother-in-law calling me to the phone. She sounded worried as she said "the doctor is on the phone". "Hello" I said, the voice on the other end of the phone said "Mrs. Griffin there has been a change in your husband's condition, someone needs to come to the hospital as soon as possible. " My legs got very weak. My husband, (Charlie) had surgery to remove one of his kidneys that morning. He had been on dialysis for about six months. Little did I know that this would be my first real challenge in life.

My brother in law came and we both rushed to the hospital. When we arrived, I remember walking down a long hall to a small waiting area. There to greet us was a chaplain, doctor, and a nurse. The doctor began to explain that complications had occurred in the recovery room.

Charlie had begun bleeding and they couldn't stop it. He had died just before we got there. I didn't know exactly how to process what was going on. Thank God my brother in law was there for me!!

We somehow made it through the funeral. Now my attention had to turn to my children. I had four girls ages five, four, two, and three months old. I was only twenty two years old. What was I to do, how was I going to care for the girls without a father? I had to drop out of school at sixteen because I had gotten pregnant. Charlie and I got married at a young age. I did not have a relationship with God at that time, but my mother in law did. I knew she was always praying for us. She would encourage me that we were going to make it. I didn't believe it at the time. After all I didn't have a high school education and never had a job before. She wasn't rich and neither was my family, what was she talking about? I just knew we would end up on welfare, because that was the way I grew up. That was my next challenge: raising my children on welfare.

I am the second oldest of sixteen children. We were very poor and had to grow up on welfare because my mother could not do any better. I knew she did the best she could, but I thought I could strive to do something different for my children. That was my driving force from that point on.

The following year I went searching for a job. I was blessed to find a job working as a Nurse's Aide at the University of Chicago Hospitals. At that time you did not need a high school diploma to work in that position. I learned to love that kind of work very much. As the years went by I began to feel something was missing in my life. I met Henry Baker and we began dating. He took a liking to my children and I was pleased with that. We got married in 1971. Henry had three sons of his own. The boys would come to stay with us periodically and the girls came to know them as their brothers.

Everything was going well, but I still felt as if something was missing in my life. I always felt bad about not completing high school. How could I tell my girls about the importance of education and I had not completed mine? As God would have it the opportunity opened up where I could get my GED. The hospital offered a program helping people get their GED and they would pay for it. I could not pass up that chance to get my diploma, so I jumped at that opportunity. I continued to work and study at the same time. I got my GED in 1973. I loved the kind of work I was doing, but I wanted to expand what I could do in nursing. I talked it over with Henry about going back to school for nursing and he was very supportive of my decision. Needless to say I did just that. So between working and going to school part-time I finally received my Associates Degree in Nursing in

1978. This was another challenge in my life that I met and overcame, thanks be to God!

My mother-in-law continued to play a very important part in my life. She was the constant influence in my children's and my own spiritual growth. She accepted Henry and his boys as her own. She took the girls to church every Sunday. When we moved away from the neighborhood, she made sure I got them to church. As I mentioned before, she had a relationship with God and she wanted to make sure we developed the same relationship with Him.

Life was going along pretty well. I had a good family, loving and supportive husband, good job and most importantly I was developing a relationship with God. What else could you ask for, right? Overtime, I began to notice that when I would get dressed for work my body would feel stiff. I still went to work but the stiffness just got worse and worse. I finally went to the doctor. He ran tests and diagnosed me with Rheumatoid Arthritis. That was a low point in my life. "God, what am I to do now?" I would pray. I loved my work and although Henry was working, we still needed my income to provide a decent way of life for my family. We just could not afford for me not to work. I began treatment and God blessed me where I could continue to work. There were days when I did not feel like going to work, but I would make it.

Henry was also very influential in the raising of the girls. We both worked two different shifts and he was available when I was not. He really stepped into the "father's role" when needed. When the girls began dating, he was there to make sure the boys they were seeing treated them appropriately. He taught them many "life" values. He loved them and they loved him. He was the only father my youngest (Yolanda) knew, after-all she was only three months old when her father died.

After my oldest daughter (Antoinette) graduated from high school and started going to college she decided to relocate to Atlanta, Georgia. At the time, I struggled with her decision. We had never been that far away from each other. However, as I reflect back I know that was the best decision she could have made. My third daughter (Cassandra) had also relocated to Georgia. So now, I had two daughters away in another state. Meanwhile, my second daughter, Inez blessed me with my first grandson and that was a joy!

When Yolanda graduated from high school and started college I decided to go back to school to get my Bachelor's Degree in Nursing. After discussing it with Henry he was agreeable to that. There were days when my arthritis would flare up but I continued to strive for that goal. I knew I could do it, after-all God had been faithful enough to see me through my other challenges in life and He would see me through this challenge. Guess what, He did! I got my Bachelor's Degree in 1991.

Several years later, my daughter Yolanda got married and blessed me with my second grandchild. She and her family then relocated in Phoenix, Arizona. She also had my third grandchild while living in Arizona. My family was expanding and moving to different states. When I think about how good God has been to me I just want to cry. He remembered a scared twenty two year old widow with four children when she prayed to Him for guidance, even though she did not have a personal relationship with Him. He was faithful enough to bless her in spite of the mistakes she made in life.

The fall of 1995, I began to have additional health challenges. I had to have both of my knees replaced. Again, I prayed "God, what now"? I knew He would take care of me, but I was getting tired of dealing with my health challenges. But again God saw me through that. I had both knees replaced in 1996. I had to take off work for about six months, but I was able to return to work in the summer of 1996.

Meanwhile, Antoinette had met a young man named Johnathan Alvarado in Atlanta. They got married and started a church, Total Grace Christian Center. They were expecting their first child when I began to experience a series of deaths in my family. I lost my mother and one of my brothers within one month of each other. The winters in Chicago were getting more and more difficult for me to deal with, so during this time I would go to Georgia to spend time with my family.

It came to a point where my health was declining so rapidly that I could no longer work, so I finally had to retire in 1999. Initially, Henry was supportive of me going to stay with the children in the winters after I retired. But in 2005, after thirty four years of marriage, the time away put a strain on our marriage and we ended up divorcing. Since that time I have relocated to Georgia.

When I look back now, I thank God for my life. I could have been a statistic; another unwed teenage mother, growing up in the inner city, and raising her children on welfare. . BUT GOD….! He knew the plans He had for my life and they were meant for my good. God has blessed me with eight grandchildren. And I now attend the church my daughter and son-in-law started over 20 years ago. My daughter, Antoinette is also doing a great work for the Lord in her own right. In fact, all of my girls are working for the Lord. My last hold-out daughter, Inez, has also relocated to Georgia. So we are all reunited in the same state and attending the same church. I am very proud of the way all of my children have pursued their education. I wonder where they get it from. GOD IS FAITHFUL!!!

"Special Memories of a Little Boy Growing Up in the Mississippi Delta"

By Bobby Moore

Growing up in the Mississippi Delta was a blessing and a curse. The Mississippi Delta was and still is one of the poorest areas in the United States of America. It is an area of land that stretches east just beyond Greenwood, MS, west to the Mississippi river, North to the Tennessee state line, and south to Vicksburg MS. We were materially poor, although I didn't realize it at that time, but by the grace of God we were rich with family love and togetherness. I was the youngest of twelve children, so I didn't get a lot of new stuff. When you are the seventh of seven boys sometimes you get stuff that's third or fourth handed. Before 1970 schools in Mississippi was segregated, and black schools weren't adequately funded. But our teachers were determined to make their students successful. When I visit my old school today and see that they now have air condition, it makes me wonder how I ever learned anything in the 90° heat, especially a couple years when I was in elementary and our school turned out early so we could chop cotton, and we had to go to school in July and August before turning out again to pick cotton in parts of September and October. But in spite of the hardship I love the South. And according to James C. Cobb the Mississippi Delta is the

99

most southern place on earth because of its unique racial, cultural, and economic history. It was one of the richest cotton-growing areas in the nation before the Civil War (1861-1865).[1] Because cotton farming was labor intensive, wealthy plantations owners depended on black slaves for labor; the Delta population well before the Civil War was and still is majority black. I left the South for a better economic opportunity, but I always knew I would return, and one of the many fond memories, I have of growing up in the Delta, were fishing trips with my mom. In 1991 I shared one of those memories with my English class.

A Fishing Trip with My Mom and Her Friend:

When I was a child growing up in the Mississippi Delta, going along on fishing trips with my Mom, Viola Moore, and her friend, Ella Howard, was one of the things I enjoying doing. In the Delta there were many man-made ditches, to drain water off the miles and miles of flat farmland after a rainstorm. These ditches were necessary if the land was to be used for farming. They were also excellent places for fishing.

On that hot Saturday morning in June when we were going fishing, I woke up without having to be called. I got up early, before the chickens roused, and went out behind the hen house and dug up some earthworms to use

---

[1] James C. Cobb, The Most Southern Place on Earth: The Mississippi Delta and the Roots of Regional Identity (1992)

as bait. There were always plenty of worms behind the hen house, because it shaded that area and prevented the sun from drying it out. While I was getting the bait, Mom and Mrs. Ella were drinking tea and preparing our lunch, peanut butter sandwiches, spiced ham sandwiches, and teacakes. With our lunch, baits, and fishing poles packed, we were ready to go.

The place where Mom and Mrs. Ella decided to go was about a mile and a half from our house, but we were going by a store to get soda waters, (pops) to drink, Bloodhound chewing tobacco for Mom, and Garrett snuff for Mrs. Ella. Going by the store added another half mile to our trip. Leaving home about seven o'clock that morning we walked along a blacktop road. I walked a few feet ahead of them, but stayed close enough to hear their conversation. I liked listening to Mom and Mrs. Ella talk because they didn't have very much school education. Because of their lack of education they couldn't use big words that I didn't understand. They used code words when they didn't want me to know what they were talking about. Mrs. Ella was telling Mom about someone who had been shot. She said, "The shot hitter right in the pocketbook, she in the hospital." That statement didn't make sense to me because at age nine or ten I knew what a pocketbook was; I knew that getting shot in the pocketbook didn't hurt people! I assumed Mrs. Ella was using gestures to help Mom understand what she was talking about, but I didn't dare turn around because I was afraid of being scolded or worse-get a spat of tobacco juice in my eyes.

Afraid to look back, I decided to slow down and let them pass me, but Mrs. Ella immediately recognized what I was doing and asked me if I was listening to grown folk talking; before I could answer Mom told me to go way ahead of them. Not being able to hear their conversation made me angry, so I begin plotting my revenge against them. Because I knew that Mrs. Ella, a short stout lady who I believed could whip most men, was afraid of everything that hopped or crawled, I waited until we were on the dirt road that ran along the number nine ditch bank where we were going fishing. The road was covered with grass above the ankles, except for the two tracks made by car tires. Mom walked in one track and Mrs. Ella walked in the other; I was walking in the track ahead of Mrs. Ella when I saw a frog in front of me. To keep from scaring it away I crossed over into the other track pretending to be looking at something on the other side of the ditch. After walking for about forty-five seconds, I was getting giddy with anticipation when I heard the scream that was the signal, which let me know the show had begun. I looked back, acting surprised, and saw Mrs. Ella jumping, trying to stay off the ground. I had to bite my lip and frown to keep them from seeing me laugh.

I liked going along when Mom and Mrs. Ella went fishing, and I liked to fish, but I was mostly along for the food and drink, and to listen to their conversation.

Whenever Mrs. Ella talked to me about her childhood, she would always say, "When I was a little boy." I thought that was funny because in the late fifties little boys didn't grow up and become women, but today it sometimes happens."

Growing up in the south in the fifties and sixties had many challenges but also many rewards. Not having money to buy toys we had to be creative, we used our minds, we made our toys; we made sling shots with shoe tongues, rubber from a bicycle inner tube, and a forked stick. We made stilts to walk on; we made telephones with two cans and a long wire or string, etc. We played family games so we had lots of family time. We ate healthy because we grew and raised much of our food.

In the Delta as a kid you had to go to church. I still remember those days at Walnut Grove M. B. Church, little sinners on mourners' bench. When you confessed if the Deacons didn't think you were sincere they would send you back to the bench. I still remember the confessions of some of my friends, "I ask God to let the sun shout"; "I ask God to give me a burning in my heart"; "I ask God to make the sun disappear under the cloud". I tried that last one myself, but I didn't believe it when it happened, and I knew I didn't have enough faith to bring a cloud from the other side of the sky. Thank God that's not what's required of us. As I look back over my life growing up in the Delta, if I could have seen where I am now I wouldn't have changed a thing!

"MENDING FENCES"

By K. Nature Mosley King

And forgive us our trespasses as we forgive those who
trespass against us; Matthew 6:12

Adults carrying hatred around is bad, children carrying
hatred (think about it for a minute) should be unheard of,
but, believe me it's real and very much alive, it can and
will happen if you have unforgivable hatred in your heart,
especially for someone that you care nothing about: a
family member.

Here's my story:

It was on May 16, 1960, when we were notified that my
mother, Ethel Mae Long Echols, had died from an
aneurysm to the brain. Living in Cincinnati, Ohio, my
mom was a young, vibrant, twenty-eight year old who
nurtured five children aging from three months to nine
years. With me being the oldest child, my mom had taught
me how to be responsible, so I became an instant mom
and my life drastically changed! My father, William
Henry Echols, Sr., made his living driving 18 wheeler
trucks so needless to say, he was on the road at the time of
mom's death. My mother was an only child, and my
grandmother lived in Newnan, Georgia. It was then that it
became real to me; my siblings and I are in Ohio, and the
only people we could rely on were our elderly aunt and
uncle on my mother's side of the family. Eventually, my
father was located, and they were able to contact his

relatives. My father's oldest sister, Mary E. Teague, immediately rushed to Ohio the day after mom passed and carried all of us to live with her in Asheville, North Carolina. The most devastating part of losing my mom was that we kids never got to say goodbye. I thought, "at least she's keeping all of us together!" In my mind, I knew we needed to stay together because like mom, I was going to die at age twenty-eight and I needed all the time with my brothers and sisters I could have. The spirit of fear gripped me, and I was counting down to 28. The closer I got to that number, the more afraid I became.

From the first day we arrived in Asheville, there was an eerie feeling that seemed to go over my body by just looking at my aunt's husband. It seemed I took an instant dislike to him, justifiably! He had a hard, mean and evil look about him...a drunk! I noticed every word that came from his mouth was profanity, or as we say, a cuss word! I still remember the first word that he said to us when we arrived in Asheville was a cuss word. With my mom passing and me dealing with the fear of also dying at twenty-eight, I knew I would not be able to tolerate him in my life. I knew that at that very moment there were going to be problems with him, and believe me there were plenty! This was the starting point of a life of pure hatred from me to him!

On our first Sunday in North Carolina, my aunt got us dressed for church. We attended church in Ohio, but this was a different kind of church. While living in Cincinnati, we attended the Catholic Church and school. In Asheville, my siblings and I were now being introduced to the Baptist faith. What a change! What a change! What a change! This church really had the juice and set it off. I was truly amazed. MOUNT ZION MISSIONARY BAPTIST CHURCH was and still is the largest Black church in Asheville. From the moment I walked into the sanctuary, I felt at home. I loved the structure of the church. It's windows throughout the church were stained glass; the pipe organ had chimes that could be heard over a large part of the city, and there was a steeple. The people greeted us with warm smiles and tight hugs. The pastor, The Reverend Doctor John W. White, was a man of integrity. There was so much to get involved in: deacons leading devotion, appointed church mothers praying prayers that you could feel and would get anyone in the spirit! I loved Sunday school, as a matter of fact everything that I learned from the Bible at my young age, I learned in Sunday school, and when I became a teen, I taught Sunday school. My favorite part of church was devotion and the music, hymns to be exact! The first hymn I remember hearing the choir sang was "I need Thee every hour, most gracious Lord. No tender voice like thine, Can peace afford. I need thee, O, I need Thee; every hour I need Thee! O bless me now, my Savior, I come to thee! I felt chills cover my body. Every Sunday, we would arrive home from church only to hear my uncle spurting dirty, filthy cuss words from his mouth. I would try to sing the hymns, but my voice was no match for the choir so I would hum each hymn. I felt like I heard God saying, "Don't worry, I Got This!" That would ease my mind until the next cussing session.

The year I arrived in Asheville, I was in fourth grade. My teacher, Ms. Louise White, was a life saver during my school years. For some unknown reason, from the first day I entered Lucy S. Herring Elementary School, she had taken a liking to me. Not only was she a mentor to me, she became personally involved in my life. Being that my aunt had my brother and sisters to care for, she unofficially adopted me. Ms. White made sure that I was involved in many school and outside activities. Girl Scouts was popular during my school year, so thanks to Ms. White, I was a Girl Scout through the twelfth grade. Everything I needed, Ms. White provided including getting my hair done and paying for my lunch. This was a huge help for my aunt. Ms. White was also my confidant. "Ms. White," I questioned one day, "why am I going through all of this mess with my uncle while I am so young?" Speaking with compassion, she warned me, "Baby, you haven't seen anything yet, just keep living!" She shared in my life until she passed away when I was 22 years old. I still miss her.

When Ms. White said "just keep living", I didn't think she meant this soon! By age eleven, I began to feel like I was being abused mentally and emotionally. I got heavily involved in church activities in order to avoid going home. My aunt didn't mind us being away from home as long as we were in church; so I made church my home as much as I could.

Even though I was in church, by age twelve, I had had enough of my uncle. This man was out of control and I felt it was my responsibility to bring him back to reality! He would never hit us (I think if he had I probably would have killed him for certain) but, the way in which he cussed us was even more painful! I was strong willed; I wasn't going to continue to tolerate his verbal abuse towards us kids. So, what did I do? I began to cuss him back! I tell you, I learned to cuss in paragraph form; no commas, no periods, just straight through, nonstop cussing! I would cuss so bad, I would have to hum the words of Horatio R. Palmer's hymn "Yield Not to Temptation", ask the Savior to help you, comfort, strengthen and keep you, He is willing to aid you, He will carry you through. Humming the words to that song would ease my spirit whenever I had to look at my uncle.

One morning, I woke up earlier than usual. The top of my sister's door frame had cracks around it. To my surprise, my uncle was standing in a chair and peeping through the cracks. I stood in astonishment for a few minutes before I could speak. I screamed, "What are you doing in that chair, and what are you looking at through those cracks?" I knew an unbelievable excuse was coming. "I was trying to see how much air was coming through the cracks. I was going to patch the cracks up so the girls would be warm." I knew he was lying. Several days back I caught him in my sister's room standing over her as she slept. His story, "I was looking for the hair grease." When I would tell my aunt, she would say, "You know he's drunk, he's not going to do anything." She would then cuss him and it was on, a cussing match! When my aunt got tired of cussing, she would get her gun, go outside, shoot into the tree and tell him the next time it would be him! He would leave and go to the liquor house for a few hours and come back drunker than the liquor itself and fall asleep for hours!

By now, my attitude was awful. During the next five to six years, my behavior became unpleasant towards him. I began to have a dark side to the point where I despised him. I added cooking, helping my siblings with their homework, combing hair, making sure they were bathed and getting their clothes ready for the next day to my list that included cleaning and ironing. My uncle would come in and do as much wickedness as he could especially when my aunt was not at home. It was those days when I would stack all of his meanness in my head and save it for the days when I would really try to do something to him. Oh, yes, I was really at the point of doing bodily harm to him! I would talk with Ms. White and she would not only listen to me vent, she would give me great advice. I would try to follow her advice, but being a teenager then was no different from being teenager today. We just went about doing things differently and we knew everything. My uncle never tried anything sexual with me except on one occasion; he kept asking me if I needed any money and while asking, he tried to hand it to me. As I looked at him, my eyes were shooting darts at his chest. I've always disliked fresh old men. I waited until dinner time that night and thought to myself, "I'm going to get him today." While I was preparing his dinner plate, I reached under the cabinet and pulled out a can of Raid bug spray and sprayed it in his soup. I wanted it to at least make him sicker than sick. When nothing happened, I was sick to the point of physically hurting. I learned later that the large amount of bootleg liquor he drank that day cut the strength of the bug spray, so the little amount that I sprayed in his soup really did not matter. The next day, he came home cussing, pulled the phone line out of the socket and turned off the television while we were watching it. I became angry and upset, so I told him I lanced his food the night before. He gave a villain type laugh and called me a lie. The look of resentment and hatred I gave him frightened my sister. She said she had never seen that look on my face before and hoped she would never see it again. I told her I felt no remorse, none whatsoever!

Hatred had taken over every part of my being. This is when I put together a plan that would totally destroy him. My next plan; I love to read, always have, so I bought a composition book and some detective magazines. Growing up, you could buy detective magazines from the newsstands. So, each month I bought a magazine and read it thoroughly. After completing the magazine, I would go back and read it again, only this time, I would write down ways to make this man non-existent. I would take notes of specific ways on how to get away with crimes involving people that you felt harmed you in any way. I continued reading detective magazines and writing notes for about two years. I wanted to have it right when I carried out the plan! No matter who I planned it with, what I planned, when I planned it, where or why I planned it, the plan could never be carried out on Wednesday evening or a Sunday. I was always in church on those days. If it was summer, I was spending time with Ms. White or working a summer job. I opened my hymnal book one day (each member bought their own book through an installment plan) and the page fell open to the hymn Yield Not to Temptation. It was then that I threw my composition book away and tried to forget my uncle. It didn't register that I also had to forgive him and myself.

I would stay away from home as much as possible. When I was home, I was doing chores. On this particular day, I was pressing clothes. Since his shirts were in the basket, I had to iron them too. As fast as I press the shirts, he would grab them and throw them on the floor. I remember telling him to go on and stop his mess, and all he did was cuss, cuss, and more cussing. When I grew tired, I grabbed the iron and laid it on the upper part of his arm. It was a nasty burn, but instead of the idiot going to the emergency room, he put butter and some type of paste on the burn. He had enough nerve to ask me to wrap it up for him! I smiled and walked away. When my aunt came home, he told her that grease from frying chicken splattered on him. She looked at him. I think she knew I burned him but she never said anything to me about it. He was ok for a while after the iron incident until one day about three weeks later. He came home again and started all over. I still ignored him. I would push his plate of food at him with so much hatred that I began to feel bad myself. I prayed to God to change my attitude. I continued to pray for change. I had to if I was going to make it in life. I went to talk with my Sunday school teacher and Ms. White. They both kept telling me that I had not fully placed not only my attitude, but my trust in God. They reminded me that until I forgave my uncle, it would grow worse by the day. And that it did! It became so bad that I had headaches, toothaches, and any other ache you could think of. I would only eat a little food if I ate at all, and began to withdraw from people. Luckily, this only lasted a short time.

It was close to graduation and I was happy. I had planned to leave my aunt's house as soon as possible. In the projects we had clothes lines to hang our clothes out to dry. We had a washer hookup but not a dryer hookup. You used the clothes line on a first come basis. This particular day, I was hanging up clothes on the clothes lines. I had gotten up early so that I could get the clothes dried, ironed and put away before the day had gone by. As

I was hanging up the clothes, my uncle came up and started to grab the clothes off the line and throw them on the ground. My mind snapped! I lost all sense of reasoning. In an instant, I picked up a fallen line, wrapped it around his neck and tried to choke him. My boyfriend lived a few doors down from my aunt's house and was on his way down to chit chat with me while I was hanging clothes. He saw my drunken uncle struggling to get the wire out of my hands. He immediately dragged me from my uncle while another guy grabbed my uncle and pushed him away from me. Again, I felt no remorse. What I did feel was that this was the last straw.

That same day I went apartment hunting and found a small studio apartment. It wasn't much but it was mine, and I would not have to look at my uncle again! I felt sorry for my siblings because they would have to stay there and listen to the cussing and his drunken rages. One of my sisters left my aunt's house at the age of sixteen and refused to ever come back and she never came back to my aunt's house. Even today, my sister continues to be mad at my aunt. My aunt called me one evening and said she wasn't feeling well; that she was having hot flashes and chest pains. She was having a heart attack. I in turn called the fire department and had them to send an ambulance to her house to take her to the hospital. She asked me to meet her there. My uncle was not at home; he was at the liquor house as usual! When I left the hospital, I had to go to my aunt's house to get some papers that the hospital needed. Not to my surprise, my uncle had made it home and he and my aunt's sister was fighting like cowboys in a saloon! My brother had picked up a bat and knocked my uncle upside the head. Someone called the ambulance but I would not let them in the house to treat him. The paramedics called the police and when they arrived they informed me that I had to let them in the house, so I did. I would go to the hospital each day to see about my aunt and never once stopped by to see my uncle, even though they were in the same hospital but on different floors. At that time, I just didn't care.

I was sitting in the hospital chapel one day praying for my aunt, and I heard words then music in my ears. I heard someone say, "That's enough; lay down all of that HATRED and FORGIVE! After all, haven't I forgiven you over and over?" The voice was so real, so strong, as if it was directly in front of me. I had the boldness to question the voice by asking, "How can I forgive this man when he's been nothing but a complete nightmare; mean and evil, disrespectful to my siblings and me. And God, You're asking me to forgive him?" The voice said in a commanding voice, "I am not asking you, I am telling you, FORGIVE this man!" At the hospital chapel, I remember going to the altar. After I left the altar, I went home and picked up my hymnal and turned to the hymn, Is Your All on the Altar. This time I didn't hum the song, I sang the words; "You have longed for peace and for faith to increase, and have earnestly, fervently prayed; but you cannot have rest or be perfectly blest until all on the altar is laid. Is your all on the altar of sacrifice laid? Your heart does the Spirit control? You can only be blest, and have peace and sweet rest, as you yield Him your body and soul." I sang all four verses and then prayed for God to forgive me for hating my uncle and take control of my life if that was His will to be done.

It still took me a few years battling back and forth with forgiving my uncle because I realized that I had to forgive ME before I could forgive anyone else. I continued to pray that one day I would be able to mend fences with him and he with me. When that day came, I went to my aunt's house and told her I needed to speak to my uncle alone. Seeing him sitting there looking like an old man that had aged twenty to thirty years, I told him three words...I FORGIVE YOU! I had sincerely forgiven him for all those years of evilness, meanness, freshness, low life ways and hurt. He looked up at me as if he didn't recognize who I was or understand what I was saying. I looked at my aunt and she informed me that he was in the early stages of dementia. Instead of feeling hatred for him, I felt sorry for him. Drops of tears were actually running down my face. The fences that were broken between my uncle and me had finally been mended. I want to think he felt the same way; that we had finally made peace with each other. I never saw him again after that day.

"See You Don't Know My Story"
By Cheryl Moon

See you don't know my story!

Filled with pain, loss, and misery,

Watching friends leave for Vietnam, never to see them return.

See you don't know my story!

Lost two nephews in a fire,

Can't help but cry to God, "Won't you take me higher?"

See you don't know my story!

Of how I met my husband,

Had three sons, moved to Georgia.

They all grew up, went off to school,

Time just seemed to pass too soon!

After graduation, some sons got married,

And then came six grandchildren.

The year I turned 50, I returned to Philly to celebrate!

My mama caught a cold,

Worried that it was something more, off to the doctors we go.

The doctor came in and said, "Her oxygen is just too low."

Little did we know, the prognosis would be grim.

Mama had cancer, the "Big C" she called it.

The doctors gave her two months to live,

But God gave her two years.

Left my husband, sons, and grandchildren to take care of my mother.

Chemo, radiation and shots in the stomach were all a part of her care.

When her body could no longer take any more,

I was there as she took her last breath.

See you don't know my story!

Through the pain, loss, and misery, I found by calling.

God placed people in my path to let me know, I was placed on this earth to care for people and to bring my calling to fruition through the joy I get from helping people during difficult times.

See you did not know my story!

*I will instruct you and teach you in the way you should go; I will counsel you and watch over you. **(Psalm 32:8)***

"That's What He's Done for Me"
By Selin Rives

The coming of another year is always so exciting, and I am on my way to church to celebrate a brand New Year. But my thoughts are troubled by the memory of a new year that was not so happy. I remember it as if it was yesterday.

It was 10:30 p.m. on New Year's night when I walked into the precinct to prepare for my 11p.m. shift. I was an Atlanta Police Officer. I got a good battery for my hand-held radio and listened to the radio traffic. As I listened, I determined that it was going to be a busy night. A short time later, I heard the dispatcher give a BOLO (be on the lookout) for a Jeep Cherokee that had just been stolen. After roll call, I got into my patrol car. Before I could inform the dispatcher that I was prepared to receive calls, a car fitting the description sped past me. It was the same jeep I had heard the dispatcher give a lookout on earlier. I ran the plates to verify that it was the same make and model. It was! The chase was on! Speeding at full force, the suspect headed north on Spring Street, and I was hot on his tail. Driving at high speed, we approached International Boulevard. Not noticing the huge bump in the road, the driver hit it and began spinning out of control. I brake hard but to no avail. The jeep struck my car causing me to lose control and spin out. When our vehicles finally came to a stop, there was a sea of blue lights and emergency vehicles. My eyes filled with tears as my mother revisited the night of such a tragic accident that changed my life forever.

The commanding officer, Major J.J. Bennett, was left the arduous task of notifying my family that I had been involved in an accident. After contacting my family, the Major and Officer Williams drove to my parents' home to provide them with transportation to the hospital. My mother, who is affectionately known as Miss Alice, and my father who was called Mr. Mike by most people who knew him, were anxiously waiting when they arrived. It was going to be a long night!

My mom will never forget the sense of foreboding she felt that night. When the policeman knocked on my parents' door to take them to the hospital, she remembered thinking, "my child needs me." When they pulled into the hospital, as far as their eyes could see were blue uniforms.

She had never seen so many policemen in one place in all of her life. My parents were not allowed to see me for a long time. They sat there for hours, until finally a young doctor came out of the room where I was being treated. The doctor was the Chief Neurologist at Grady Hospital. He told them something they already knew- that I was a fighter. He assured them I was in there fighting for my life. He went into details with them as to how I had suffered thirteen seizures and that I was now in a coma. He explained that I had suffered serious head trauma, but he was unable to say how much at this time. While the doctor was talking, there was no sound coming from his lips to my mom because she just needed to see her child. Finally, she held up her hand and asked him when they could see me. He told my parents that they were moving me to the Intensive Care Unit at that very moment, and as soon as I was in my room he would take them in to see me. When the doctor came out to take them to my room, he explained a few more things to them. He said that patients who are in a coma still have the ability to hear, therefore, they should talk about positive things when they were around me.

When mom and dad walked into the room, mom was looking down at the bandaged, bruised, and swollen face of a person who did not resemble her child. My head had been shaved clean and there was a scraggily line of stitches on the left side. There was a tube in my mouth because the doctor said that I was not breathing on my own. There were all kinds of machines beeping, blinking, and making noises, and it looked just like I was sleeping. I didn't move even when my dad said my name. I just laid there sleep. Mom and dad stood there for a long time just staring at me, silently praying that I would move, hoping that I would snap out of it and look up at my daddy with my silly grin that the two of us shared – I did not.

By lunchtime, my mom couldn't take it anymore, so she told dad that she had to go home and check on Andre' and Justin, my sons, and give an update to the others. My dad stayed at the hospital with me while an officer took mom home. During the ride home, the dam of tears broke, and my mom cried uncontrollably. She felt so alone, and her child was at the point of death. She was still crying when calm washed over her, and she knew right then that His grace was sufficient for me and for her. When my mother arrived home, she found her house filled with members from the church we attended, and all of my siblings – Carl, Carla, Tina, and Valerie, were all waiting. Every eye in the house was on mom.

Meanwhile, mom was sitting in that hospital room alone with me and everything seemed so surreal. She expected for somebody to come and wake her from this awful nightmare, but nobody came. Out of all of their kids, she remembered, I had always been the adventurous one. I was always the leader, checking things out, and too often getting into tons of trouble. Looking at me then, she didn't want to see that bandaged woman lying there in that hospital bed. She wanted to see that little girl who had investigated a big, gray ball hanging from the tree with the hole in it in the back yard. I had led the way, with my sisters and brother following closely behind me. I put a stick up and stirred it around in the dark hole for just a couple of seconds. It only took a couple of seconds to stir up the hornets that were inside the gray ball before they attacked us. Needless to say, I and my siblings found out what the gray ball was before that day was over; we were all covered with a black cloud of hornets as we made a mad dash for the house! Now, this same adventurous little girl was laying there looking as though she was sleeping peacefully.

Days turned into weeks, and weeks turned into months. The tube that was in my throat was removed, along with many of the machines. Finally, one morning in March, a nurse from the hospital called the house and said that I was awake. My parents got over to the hospital as fast as they could. When they arrived at the hospital, my doctor was in the room with me. Dad was the happiest man on earth! When I looked over at him and gave my goofy grin, it felt like old times. My mother walked over to my bed, took my hand as I tried to speak. That's when mom knew everything was not all right. I glanced at her with a distressful look on my face and muttered, "D-d-da-daddy m-m-my h-h-h-head hurts." I tried to raise my hand to my head, but it was as though my hand was made of lead. I did not seem to have the strength to lift it up. My hand began to twitch a little bit, and then my whole body began to jerk uncontrollably while my eyes rolled to the back of my head. The medical staff got everyone out of my room so quickly; none of them knew what was happening.

Mom and dad waited for hours before the attending physician came out to speak to them. She informed them that I had experienced a seizure. In fact, I had three consecutive episodes. The doctor further explained to them that seizures happen when normal brain patterns are interrupted, and they have in some way become distorted, which can lead to convulsions. "This is what has happened to your daughter, Lynn," the doctor added. At the moment, I was heavily medicated and the seizures caused me to be lethargic. The doctor continued to explain that I would have to undergo a battery of tests in order to determine how much brain damage I had suffered as a result of the accident. The doctor's next statement didn't make sense to my parents; "She doesn't remember having the accident!" "And furthermore," the doctor informed them, "I am unsure of how much of Lynn's memory is affected at this point, but Lynn may be a little different."

In the coming weeks, my parents saw a few distinct changes in me that were very different from the person they knew before the accident. I stuttered very badly and always had excruciating headaches. Deep down I was still the same person. Walking back into my room one morning after getting coffee from the cafeteria, my mom saw the funniest thing- my nurse was attempting to brush my teeth, but I refused to open my mouth! The nurse tried to coax me by saying, "Now Miss Rives, you don't want your visitors to smell your breath do you?" I looked at the nurse and stuttered back, "Th-th-they are n-n-n- not g-g-going t-t-to g-g-get c-c-close enough t-t-t-to smell m-m-my b-b-b-breath." The nurse and my mom roared with laughter, even I laughed. After watching the ineffective attempts by the nurse a little while longer, my mom told the nurse that she would brush my teeth.

A few days later, my dad was at the hospital visiting me, and witnessed a very different scene. He walked in while I was with my mother. I was crying uncontrollably. Now, normally my mom is a strong woman, but this time even she was crying. Dad walked over to me and with great concern asked me what was wrong. I looked at him and said in a childlike voice, "D-d-da-da-daddy all of m-m-my hair is g-g-g-gone," and I continued to bawl. In all that had happened, my father had forgotten that I did not remember the accident, and I definitely didn't understand why I was in the hospital. My mother gently left the room and a few minutes later she returned with a bonnet she purchased from the hospital's gift shop. She put it on my shaved head and it seemed to please me! Soon after, I was asleep. My mom bought me different color bonnets, and I always wore one until my hair grew back.

After nearly four months in the hospital, it was finally time for my parents to take me home. Unable to care for myself or my boys, I went home with my parents. Little did we know the journey was just beginning! Before leaving the hospital, the doctors educated my family on some things. They told them that my equilibrium had been affected, and this would cause me to be unsteady for a while. I would need some help getting around. They also explained that I would have problems remembering things from one second to the next.

I slept most of the day, but I was awake when it was time for everyone to eat dinner. Mom fixed my plate and was about to bring it into my room when there was a loud noise that sounded as if someone was hitting on the walls. Dad went to investigate and realized that the noise was me trying to walk into the kitchen. I resembled a toddler who was learning to walk for the first time –take a few steps, fall down and try it again. Except, I was not a toddler, I was a grown woman. The sight nearly brought dad to tears. My dad wanted to help, so he reached down to grab me. In a stuttering voice, I quickly said, "I-I-I c-c-c-can d-d-d-do it d-d-d-daddy!" He walked next to me trying to help me up when I fell. It took quite a while for me to make it to the table, but nothing the doctors said could have prepared my family for what happened next. I sat down in the chair and all of a sudden I fell. Uncle Carl and dad helped me back into the chair. I sat up for less than a second, and then I would start leaning. I was like a Weeble toy, except I didn't wobble, I simply fell over again. That's when he remembered what the doctors had told them about my equilibrium. So, they gave me a chair that had arms on both sides and used a belt from a bathrobe to tie around my waist to help anchor me in the chair. Now I was able to somewhat sit in the chair without falling onto the floor. They had concocted a workable highchair for an adult.

That was only the first hurdle we had to get over! The entire time I was in the hospital, I had been fed intravenously or had eaten soup or gelatins, but I had never eaten solid foods. This was not something that had been given thought to nor had the doctor warned us about. When mom sat the plate of food before me, the results caught everybody by surprise. I had trouble picking up my fork and holding it. After a few missed tries, my son, Andre', placed the fork in my hand. I held my fork and stared at it. To me it was a foreign object that was as heavy as lead! Finally, I made an attempt at picking up some macaroni and cheese. I had no control over my fine motor skills, so most of it fell off the plate. I was learning to feed myself as if it was the first time. After much time had passed, I was able to get some food onto my fork and lifted it up to my mouth. I didn't put the fork in my mouth, I stuck the fork in my cheek near my ear; then I stuck it near my nose; and finally after a few more attempts at finding my mouth I put the food in my mouth. I was embarrassed so I put the fork down and picked up my chicken. It took a while to find my mouth again, but I did a little better with the finger foods. My mother tried to feed me when I would let her, but I was stubborn and had my pride – even if it was misplaced. When dinner was over, I had eaten three helpings of macaroni and cheese, collard greens w/cornbread, and four pieces of chicken. There were scraps of food all over the table and chair where I had been sitting, and the floor had to be swept and mopped because it was loaded with gobs of food.

"Every day was a new adventure with Lynn," my mom proclaimed! "Once I walked into Lynn's room while she was asleep to check on her and she told me to get down because they were shooting at us. When I woke her up, she just looked at me like I was from another planet until she realized who I was!" "H-h-hey m-ma-ma-ma-mama," she whispered and then went back to sleep. When I was asleep, in my mind I was always on police duty. The police psychologist explained that this was the only time that I felt I was in charge. He warned my family not to be too alarmed by my actions because I had been through a great deal. One quiet, still night as everyone was sleeping, there came a sudden loud pounding and banging noise and someone yelling at the top of their voice. My mom shook my dad and told him to get up. Dad got up, and my mom was right behind him running down the hallway trying to find out what was going on. Tina and Carl had gotten out of their beds and they were running too. Justin and Andre' were both standing at the door of their bedroom afraid to come out. There standing in the hallway in my pajamas was me banging on the wall and yelling repeatedly to an invisible perpetrator, "Put your hands on the wall!" It took a long time for daddy to wake me up because I was trying to arrest him and place his hands behind his back. After a while, my dad was able to calm me down and ultimately get me back into bed.

There were other times at night that the house would awake to a different sound. It would be the sound of moaning or the thud of someone falling out of the bed. The first time it happened was the scariest because none of the family had ever experienced anything like that before. Low moaning sounds were coming from my room one night, and mom came in to check on me. What she found scared her to death. I was having a seizure. She ran back to her room to tell my dad to dial 911 to get an ambulance. She came back to my room, and witnessed my whole body shaking out of control. I was biting my tongue, and my eyes were rolled back in my head. She stayed with me so I would not fall out of the bed or hit my head because I still had those stitches. At last, my body rested limp and lifeless and I heard the whaling of the ambulance siren. Within minutes we were on our way to the hospital. My parents would make a lot of trips like this one with me.

It's really funny how we can be really good at some things and horrible at others. When my sisters and I were younger, as a parent, my mother tried to introduce us to all kinds of things. So, we all took piano lessons and learned to play, but my natural gifting was not as a pianist, but singing. When my sons were younger, I would sing to them all the time. When they were babies, I would sing as I fed them; I would sing to them when they cried; and I would sing to lull them to sleep. As they grew older, I would sing with them to teach them different things or just for fun. Music was always a part of my identity. As a matter of fact, when I was younger and needed to be punished, my mother would take away my privilege of listening to the radio for a few days. That punishment was devastating to me, with an extremely effective outcome. So, it was never unusual or out of character to hear me break out in a song when I was in my room, but I had not been singing since the accident – it had been nearly a year now.

I was in my room with my boys one Sunday afternoon after they came home from church. I was not quite ready to go to church yet because I could not stay awake or sit up that long. Andre' and Justin were singing one of the songs that they had sung in the children's choir for me, when I joined in with them. It was the most beautiful sound my mom had heard in a long time because it signified that her daughter was home. The three of us sounded so good singing together. Then my dad came into my room and asked me to sing one of the songs that I used to sing when I was in the choir. I started to sing for my father perfectly, never stuttering once. With tears in his eyes, he listened to his daughter's rich vocal prowess as I sang for my father. My dad was amazed because I could not remember what happened ten seconds ago, but I could remember all of the words to "Jesus is the Answer", a song I sang years ago. It's just amazing!

After going through intensive speech therapy, physical therapy, occupational therapy, and psychotherapy, I was finally able to walk and speak more clearly. It took a lot more time before I was able to care for myself and my kids. I still don't remember everything, that's why my parents had to tell me my story. What I know is that through it all God was healing my body; He was right there to protect and keep me. My testimony is I've been blessed. I believe God will always make a way. Look what He's done for me!

"The Coldest Day of My Life"
By Edna Wise

July 1997 was one scorching hot month in Atlanta. My husband, daughter and I had just returned from a family reunion in Rochester, NY when I noticed a change in my daughter's speech and facial expressions. That night when she went to bed she did not rest well because she was coughing as though she were congested. The very next morning I called the doctor and was told to bring her in. The doctor diagnosed her with bronchitis because of the mucus in her throat and chest. He gave us a prescription and we were on our way. She appeared to be fine until bedtime. When she went to bed that night she coughed and gagged all night. When day light approached she appeared to be fine. I called the doctor and explained what she had done that night. They gave me an appointment for the next day. About that time she was slurring in speech. Her facial expressions had changed because she had lost her smile and had droopy eyes. This day had turned into the coldest day in July.

Worried that something terribly wrong was happening to my daughter, I took her back to the doctor. When he saw her he immediately called a Neurologist at Eagleston Children's Hospital. The doctor diagnosed her with a neuromuscular disorder called Myasthenia Gravis. At that time it was known to be a rare deadly disease. Her muscles were so weak. The mucus and secretion in her throat would just lay there in the gap. She would cough but her throat muscles were too weak to swallow or cough it up. This experience really changed my life. The thought of seeing my child looking in the bathroom mirror crying because her smile was no longer there, was heartbreaking for me. At that moment I realized just how much we take for granted. Just imagine not being able to smile. That experience made me smile more than ever.

My daughter was a very strong little girl and she had no desire to give up. Late one evening I was taking her to the hospital to be admitted and she said she felt fine. Instead of going to the hospital she wanted to stop at Sanrio to get a toy. When we got back to the car she was so weak in her trunk muscles she could not get in the car. To make matters worse, I could not lift her into the car because she had gained a significant amount of weight due to the medication she was taking. Consequently, we had to stand in the rain and regroup for the second try, but again, she was too weak. We were standing in the rain, exhausted from our unfruitful attempts, when a young couple walked toward us in the parking lot. I proceeded to ask the couple for their help but my daughter refused, she wanted to do it on her own. She made her third attempt to get in the car and the couple and I just helped her in. We then went straight to Eagleston.

The next day the neurologist ordered the Red Cross to come in to do a blood plasmapheresis, which is a procedure where the affected plasma or antibodies is removed and replaced with good plasma. After the treatment she was strong, smiling and back to school. Unfortunately, two weeks later she was weak again and her smile was gone. We went through this cycle for several months until Dr. Slackey decided to take her thymus gland out. At this time she was so weak and sick that she came down with pneumonia and had to be moved to the ICU. When she got over the pneumonia she had another plasmapherisis.

Late that evening while my daughter was having this procedure, a friend of the family called and asked me to read John 11:2 because my baby was at the point of death. I immediately grabbed my Bible and read that scripture and the chapter before and after that scripture. The scripture said, "This sickness is not unto death, but to the glory of God, that the son of God may be glorified through it." I continued to read the passage and saw how Mary and Martha had placed a limit on God after their brother Lazarus had died.

Early one Thursday morning, the technicians came to the hospital room to take my daughter to get a porch in so that she could get another plasmaphersisi, which would make her strong enough for the Thymus Gland Surgery. They had a hard time getting the porch in the groin area so they put it in the chest area. I waited impatiently because it was taking longer than normal. They finally brought her back to the room and the Red Cross was there ready to give her the treatment. As we were sitting there, her heart rate was going up and suddenly she coded. Doctors and nurses rushed in with machines. My whole body became cold as ice. I left out of the room and sat in an empty room next to hers. All I could see were people running and rushing with machines and equipment. I heard them calling my husband at his job, telling him to have someone bring him to the hospital. I got up and walked outside. When I came back in I asked the nurse, "how is my baby?" The nurse looked at me with tears in her eyes and said, "At this time we don't have a heart rate". They called the chaplain in to pray with me, but I could not wait. I went to the chapel to pray. I knelt down at the altar and earnestly began praying, "Lord I'm not Mary nor am I Martha. They put a limit on you, but I will not. I know if you went to the grave and raised Lazarus up after being dead for four days, I know you can raise little Shambreia." Immediately, a load fell off my shoulder and I turned around to walk out the chapel. As I walked out I met a nurse getting off the elevator saying, "go see your baby." When I got to the floor the doctors informed me that she would be brain dead if she lived, nonetheless, she was a miracle.

After speaking with the doctors, I walked into my daughter's room and saw machines and tubes everywhere. I looked at her little bruised body lying there on the bed and I called out her name. She opened her eyes once and then went back to sleep. I knew that she had been raised from the dead and this was truly a Lazarus experience.

A couple of nights later, as she was recovering, she threw that same little toy I stopped to get her on our way to the hospital over on me as I tried to sleep. She said, "I have a song in my mind and I can't stop singing." I asked her what song? She replied, "Jesus loves me." That was confirmation for me that she would be alright. In that moment I was reminded of my pastors' encouragement to learn the songs of the church because one day all you might have is a song.

Two weeks later she had the surgery and recovered quickly. In three months we were weaning her off of all of the medications. At age 26 years old, the little girl who went through so much has not had any complications or any medication since. She is married and has two beautiful girls. Through it all we stood on God's word and kept a song in our hearts.

"THE CROSSROADS IN LIFE"

By Connie Thomas

I am the ninth child born to Willie Mae and L. C. Adkins. As my siblings and I grew older we faced a lot of challenges, but through it all, our mother never left us, she never gave any of us away, nor did she abort us. She did what she had to do to make sure we were taken care of. I can remember going to school with a piece of cardboard inside my shoes to keep my feet from touching the ground. My underwear and socks were so dirty. I can never remember brushing my teeth until I was a teenager. We would wipe them with a towel or our finger with baking soda. We ate an abundance of rice, beans, and grits but we never went without food. It may not have been something that we wanted everyday but we would always have something to eat. I remember one day my brother Bill and I went to school and told the teacher that we did not have anything to eat so that we could just have something different. Little did we know CPS (Child Protective Services) would come to our home. When we got home our mom let us have it.

Things were so uncomfortable at home that when I was at school I really wasn't at school. My body was there but I would just stare out the windows. There were times that we would come home and our belongings were setting out on the streets. We would have gotten evicted because the landlord found out how many children there were in the apartment or the rent had not been paid. These were the things I thought about while I was in school. Needless to say, I was not able to focus on my school work and I stopped going as soon as I could.

Later in life my mother met Mr. Ceal. I think he was married but he helped her a lot. He never stayed the night but he was around for years. I thank God for him because with him around we stopped getting evicted.

When I was a teenager Eddie Winters came into our lives and he married my mother. We moved to 710 W. 60th Street in Chicago. There were two bedrooms and ten children were still living at home. We stayed at this address longer than any other place. We moved there in February 1968 and stayed until 1970. During this time I met Lawrence Thomas. My sister Willa Bea and I would be sitting on the front porch watching him walk down the street. I thought he was good looking. He was tall, dark, thin, a little bowlegged, and he had a head full of hair. I kept looking at him but my sister said that he was too old for me so I left him alone. Then one summer day we were playing ball in the streets and Lawrence stopped me right across the alley from where I lived. He asked me if I would be his lady and I responded that he did not have a chance, so he left. I guess I was looking for someone who did not look so old, especially since my sister was telling me that he was too old for me. Then I met Eugene Thompson, but he had eyes for someone else so I went over to Deloris' house and what do you know, Deloris is

Lawrence's sister. Lawrence and I met again, only this time we talked a little more. Having been recently rejected, we played checkers for a kiss and that opened the door to our relationship. What I should have been looking for was a door to school, but I guess I was just looking for love and we did fall in love. But as time went on, I found that we fell in love a little too young because we went to hell and back and I mean to HELL and back!

Lawrence and I started dating each other on December 28, 1968. I had just turned 14 that November. We did the things that teenagers do; hugging, kissing, etc. In May of 1969, we arranged a time to have sex for the first time. From that day forward it was me and him against the world! In September 1969, Lawrence went away to the army but that was short-lived because he could not seem to follow orders nor could we stand being away from each other. While he was away I met a young man named James Williams but our relationship did not go anywhere. I thought I may have gotten pregnant by him but it turned out that I wasn't. Later, I got back with Lawrence when he came back from the Army. We continued to love each other and had two beautiful daughters. In 1971, we moved into our own apartment which was below his mother's apartment. We were not there very long. Although Lawrence worked, he did not make enough to pay the household bills; so in an effort to make ends meet, we sold weed.

Lawrence had a sister named Geena who was separated from her husband and was staying with their mother until she was able to get her own place. Genna got her own apartment around 1972/73 on Harper Street but she was off into books that she should not have been into. She came over one night and brought books on witchcraft. She kept trying to get Lawrence to read the books but he responded by trying to show her things in the Bible. After much persuading, he finally gave in and read a little bit but he kept telling her that he did not want to read anymore. However, Genna kept pressuring him to keep reading to the point that Lawrence started crying. She then turned to me, wanting to read my palm. I let her know that I did not believe in this, but I said okay so she would leave Lawrence alone. She took my palm in her hand and read that something would happen to me in the year 1973 that I would remember for the rest of my life. Well, about three weeks later in May 1973, I was shot three times, in my jaw, neck and shoulder by Lawrence. When I came to after being shot, my oldest daughter was sitting on the floor next to me. A small voice came to me to tell me that I was not dead and to get up. I grabbed my daughter and ran up the stairs to Lawrence's mother's house. Lawrence got locked up for the shooting. Now here I was left with two small girls, no education, an apartment, and a pile of bills trying to figure out how I was going to make ends meet. All I knew to do was to continue to sell weed. I eventually got a job at a packing factory. The job did not last long, but I was able to keep my apartment for about a year and then I moved back into my mom's house.

Lawrence was released in September of 1974 from jail but he had to go to the Callen Maddens Mental Hospital in Maywood IL. I had to catch the bus and train from 134th Street to Maywood, IL four times a week just to see him. He was released from there in December 1974. At this point we started our life again together as a family. Yes, there were people saying, "How are you going to stay with this man who shot you three times, took another person's life and hurt your child?" My mom, mother-in-law, and my friends worried a lot about my decision to stay with Lawrence, but I had a feeling in my spirit that I needed to stand by and stay with him. I also felt that God chose me to do this. I knew it was God because only He could do something like this. I never feared that Lawrence would harm us. I also knew with all my heart and soul that Lawrence did not have any intentions to take his sister's life because he loved her more than anyone would ever know. In January 1978 Lawrence and I got married. We went through the fire together but God kept us under the shadow of His wings. In the beginning of our marriage we got lost into the world of drugs. We both did crack cocaine in 1989. I found that Lawrence had a drug habit that was taking him away from the family, so I talked to God and told Him that I wanted to save our marriage. Little did I know that I could not save anything or anybody! God let me find out on my own. I told God if Lawrence wanted to go down then I would go down with him. I was truly hoping that Lawrence would say, "No, you are the mother of my children and my wife and I don't want you to do this". But he didn't so I went and I smoked right alongside him from October 1989 until September 1995. For those 6 years, we were spinning out of control. I remember one day while at work, I could not stop crying. One of my patients asked me what was wrong and I told him that every time I make ten steps forward it seemed like I would take twenty steps backward. He told me that if I would seek God and all His righteousness that all else would be added unto me. That night, I looked up *Matthew 6:33*, which was the scripture my patient shared with me. Now, everything did not change right then but it was the beginning of a new life.

The next Wednesday night, I made my way to Salem Baptist Church of Chicago. I was so broken but I felt so comfortable and loved. That night I joined the church. I realized I had been looking for love in all the wrong places but now I was in a place where I could experience God's love. One night I cried out to God after spending $500.00 on soap, candy, chalk and Alka Seltzer which I thought was drugs. I saw God turn crack into everything except something that could kill us. God truly had His Hand on us and for this we will always give Him praise. After I cried out to God it was like He showed up and showed out. It was like the Holy Spirit started leading me around and guiding me, but there would be one last time that I did not listen to His lead.

I got high with Lawrence one more time. After the crack we started fighting. My face was so disfigured that my children were overwhelmed. They went out and called my youngest daughter, Terri and she came over with a gun and ordered me to come with her. She told her dad that this would be the last time the he would put his hands on me. She took me to the hospital where they took pictures and called the police. When we went to court I did not press charges against Lawrence. However, I left him for about three months; long enough for God to really do a work in and through me, which is what He did. I left my sons at my daughter's house and I went to a shelter. My things were rummaged through at the shelter. I was ready to leave but I knew I could not go back to my daughter's house yet. My oldest daughter, Madonna and her mother-in-law took me into their house for about three months. She put me in her back bedroom and God truly moved. I never went to a rehab center because I didn't want to deal with the red tape or have a record kept on me. I did not want to be known as the one who had a drug habit, so I went to God in prayer and He sent me to Salem Baptist Church of Chicago. The pastor of the church, Pastor James T. Meeks, never spoke to me one-on-one, he may not have known me personally, but his church was a safe haven for me. God chose to send me to dwell in His temple and to hear His Word coming from Pastor Meeks' mouth, long enough to take root in my heart. I knew how to pray, but I did not know that I should end my prayer "In Jesus Name". When I finally got that part right it was like the heavens opened up and God said, "My child you finally got the key". In three months of being in God's presence, He redeemed my soul. I never went back to crack but I did go back to my husband. My children were worried about me going back but I told them not to trust me but to trust God. I don't believe God cleaned me up to set me on a shelf like a trophy or to lock me up. He cleaned me up to send me out to let His light shine in and through me. So that is what I did. , I went back to the dope dealers and instead of asking for crack, I gave them a track and shared my story with them. My husband also was set free from his addiction. Eventually, we moved into a two-family flat.

My mom was going through hell trying to help my brother who had fallen into drugs. I remember her calling me one night and asking if I could go out and look for him because she had not heard from him in about a week. His wife and I went out looking for him on the east side of Chicago. We did not find him so I took his wife home. By the time we arrived at her house he was on the phone. I asked to speak to him. He was a very smart young man, one of the only boys of nine to complete high school. He would always speak in riddles and he would say, "If you give a man a fish you will only feed him for a day but if you teach a man to fish you will feed him for a lifetime." So I asked him on the phone that night to let me teach him to fish by calling on the name of Jesus. He cried and said that he did call on the name of Jesus but that it was not working. In October 1996 our dear mother passed away. By that time Tony had gotten lost again. I went looking for him and discovered that he had signed himself into

Methods Hospital where I was working at the time. We got him out in time for the funeral service and I told him he could stay with us, but he had to promise not to steal from us; he had a bad habit of ripping you off while you were asleep. He agreed. A week went by and one day when I came home my back door had been broken in and Tony was just laid up with his hands behind his head as if nothing had taken place. I asked him what happened; he looked at me and said that he did not know; that it broken when he woke up. I asked him to leave before Lawrence and my son got off work. I knew there would be trouble when they found out what happened. He asked if he could stay until 3 p.m. when someone would be there to pick him up. I went and sat on the front porch, smoking a cigarette and the Holy Spirit spoke to me "Ask him where his meds are". He showed me a bottle and I asked where the other one was – it was empty. I told him that he needed to leave and go to St. Bernard Hospital before he fell. Three days later my brother was found dead in an abandoned building about five blocks from my house. He was died two weeks after my mother passed. I almost lost it! They did an autopsy on him and said that they did not find anything in his system. His body had not deteriorated so you know that the Holy Spirit really had to comfort me in this and He did. You see my brother loved animals so God allowed me to see my brother as a little boy running and playing, doing just what he loved doing. It was in a dream that I saw my brother running in a tall field of grass tossing a stick to his dog and smiling like I hadn't seen him in a long time. God let me know that we didn't have to go out looking for him on cold winter nights anymore because he was in heaven now. ,

God has truly been a father, provider, protector, healer, deliverer and keeper of my family. Despite the ups and downs my family and I faced, God has seen us through. At every crossroad in my life, God has shown His light on my path so that I know which direction to go.

"Then Sings My Soul"

by Vanessa M. Goode

TRANSPARENT: able to be seen through: easy to notice or understand: honest and open: not secretive.

That's how I describe myself as I sat nervously in the crowded lobby of the doctor's office. You see, I had talked myself into believing that my rapid heartbeat and my elevated blood pressure were caused by my anticipation of seeing the doctor. Let me be transparent with you-I was scared! I knew God was with me and He had everything under control, but at that one moment, it seemed as though time had stopped and I was stuck in a place of 'what ifs'.

Months had passed since I had gone to the doctor. I wanted to see why any and everything I ate came back up.

"Mrs. Goode," the doctor explained, "you have what we call 'acid reflux'."

So, medication and change in diet. I can do that, I told myself! Little did I know that was just the beginning.

The pain continued, but now it was coming more frequently. There was this sick feeling in the pit of my stomach-a feeling that something was seriously wrong. Stress of going to work day after day and dealing with the raging hormones of know-it-all middle school students was a tremendous factor behind me feeling so bad! I mean, twelve year olds who don't like their moms, and to them, I represented that very authority figure whom they had left at home! I was not very persuasive.

After several returns to the doctor, I was not convinced that what I was experiencing was acid reflux. As a matter of fact, my condition worsened to where I felt as though I was vomiting rivers of water. Lunchtime was to be dreaded! I would describe my digestive system as having a small creature at the top of my stomach that caught my food and threw it back at me! I hated the thought of twelve-o-five!

Unexpectedly, because of the vomiting, I was rushed to the emergency room. People with flushed faces from high temperatures, sounds of deep coughing that seemed like their very insides were fighting to get out, filled the small waiting room. I sat there, gagging and sometimes vomiting at the smell of the sicknesses, hoping that I will be called next. Then I heard the magic words, "Vanessa Goode!" My husband held me tightly lifting me from the chair.

The wait in the examining room was just as tiring as the wait outside. The nurse came in periodically to check on me, reassuring me that the doctor would be in soon. I concluded that the definition of soon is when the more serious conditions are tended to! Finally, the doctor came in to see me. I have never understood why we have to tell five people the same thing! I was very irritated. In my mind I was thinking, "Can't you ask one of the five persons I've told"?

The doctor determined that she needed to look in my stomach. Without hesitation, I agreed! The procedure was completed and three to four doctors crowded around my bed.

"Mrs. Goode, we found a tumor in your stomach. We are going to do a biopsy to make sure it's not malignant." My heart dropped. It was as though a ton of bricks had come crashing down on me. I was admitted to the hospital not knowing what was ahead of me.

The doctors entered my room the next morning. My husband and children were in the room with me. She told me she had the test results, and asked if I wanted my children to leave the room. I said no. As it turned out, the tumor was cancerous. The doctor immediately suggested surgery to remove the growth, and I agreed. After the doctor exited, there was complete silence with the exception of the sniffling of noses and silent tears. We gathered ourselves and my husband prayed. God has this under control. For the first time, I was facing something that was totally out of my control!

I underwent an MRI to see if the cancer had spread to any other organs. The wait for the result felt like an eternity! Thank God that none of the organs had been affected. Now, I had to face the long, tedious journey of chemotherapy.

Nausea, vomiting, weight lost, low white blood counts-the chemo was wearing me down! God, where are you? The intercessors were interceding for me through prayer. God brought me through the horrific experience and I was cancer free!

Back to the heart-warming task of teaching one hundred twenty hormonal twelve year olds! Things were looking up for me. I had strength and energy again! I could travel back and forth throughout the school without stopping every fifteen feet to catch my breath.

Six months into the school year and life was considered to be a bowl of cherries-sweet! I was teaching on the grade level which I preferred and was working with a great team of teachers. Now, time for my routine scan rolled around. The scan went well, and I was scheduled to get the results the following week. Greg was scheduled to work, but there was this urgency deep in my soul for him to go with me. "Good morning, Mrs. Goode," the pleasant voices rang out. "How are you this morning?"

"I'm doing great!" I responded, trying to return the positive attitude.

"The doctor will be with you soon."

Soon, a doctor whom I was not familiar with entered the room. I'm not sure if he introduced himself before he started to question me as to how I was feeling. He didn't waste any time getting to the results of the scan. "Mrs.

Goode, the cancer has returned on both lungs." It's almost as though he had no emotions as he delivered this devastating news to me. In a split second, my whole world came crashing down on me! My mind went blank; it felt like the very breath was leaving my body. For the first time I knew what it meant to not be able to pray. I wish I could say that I called the devil a lie, went off in spiritual tongues and threw up the victory sign, but I didn't. I had heard testimonies from the saints of how when they received bad news, they immediately started to pray. They would witness to how God bought the answer before they could get up from their altar. But instead, I sat there in my husband's arms in disbelief and wondering "why is this happening to me?" The doctor explained to me that the cancer was inoperable. So as to not give me false hope, he informed me that chemotherapy would only manage the tumors.

Lord, I need a miracle! I am being transparent-I want to live! Months passed and even though the tumors were shrinking, they were still there. Whenever Elder Marsha would see me, she would assure me that she and the intercessors were keeping me lifted up in prayer. People were testifying of the miraculous healing of God.

On this particular Sunday, Apostle Scale ministered in the service. He had a massive altar call for those who needed something from God. My legs were as weak as water and were shaking like a leaf in the fall. My daughter helped me to the front. I had been in prayer lines so many times, but this time seemed different. As I sat on the altar, Co-Pastor Dr. Toni, came down, laid hands and prayed with me. Umm, I didn't feel electricity go from the top of my head to the sole of my feet, nor did I fall out under the power! But God was still working.

I looked around the waiting room of the doctor's office, My blurry eyes were fixated on the many people who had been affected by this disease-ladies who were bald as results from the chemo, men in wheelchairs because their bodies were weaken by medication and disease. Asians, Whites, Blacks, Hispanics, young and old, and me! I actually thought that because I served the Lord, I was excluded from such devastation! This big "C" has no respect of person.

It was my turn to see the doctor. I expected the routine conversation of "how do you feel today? How has your appetite been? And of course, "the tumor is shrinking"! "Good morning Mrs. Goode," the Nurse Practitioner greeted me. "How are doing today?" I responded truthfully to her question. "Well, this tingling in my hands and feet are driving me crazy!"

She gave me a slight smile and it was time to get to the results of the scan.

"Mrs. Goode, I wanted to be the one to give you the results of your scan."

I glanced at my husband who was sitting on the edge of his chair in the corner of the room. "Okay, let's have it," I said as my voice dropped.

"Your scan is perfect!" She said with this huge glowing smile on her face.

I couldn't believe what I was hearing! "Could you repeat that?" "There are no lesions on any of the organs. It's a perfect scan." I couldn't hold back the praise and worship! My husband and I praised God right there in the presence of the Nurse Practitioner. God had worked a miracle in my life. Now I can say I testify to what God will do.

To be transparent for me was to take my situation to the altar and admit to God that I was broken, afraid and not in control. That was the place He wanted me to be. I wish I could say that the journey was over, it's not. But the joy of The Lord is my strength and I now know first-hand that no matter what I go through, the battle is not mine but the Lord's.

My soul sings, How Great Thou Art!

"THROUGH THE STORM"

By Ronnie Thompson

I can remember the day that changed my perspective on life as if it were branded into my mind just yesterday. It was a normal Saturday morning, you know the one you look forward to every Friday and the one you start planning for on Monday morning. It had also been gruesome at work that week where so many things were not going right, and it seemed that nothing was going according to plan. I remember that Saturday morning distinctly.

As it was my normal routine on Saturday morning, I got up early that particular day and was just lying around planning to do nothing all day. I deserved it. I mean I was the head of the household, and had completed my required provider duties for the week and today was going to be my day. I earned this day to be a couch potato and watch whatever was on the tube all day. I remember hearing that old familiar sound of the squeaking stairs as my wonderful two children came running hurriedly down the stairs, and I remember thinking "I sure hope those kids don't slip and fall down the stairs" because it happened to my daughter before. She often teases me now about that time she tumbled down the stairs and I said to her "you better not have broken my railings." We still laugh about that.

Of course my son, the musician destined for greatness, was already downstairs in the basement practicing on the drums. We were a normal family household with a very nice home God had blessed us with, and we were so proud of what he was doing in our lives.

During that particular time in our life my brother-in-law from Durham, North Carolina was living with us while he attended school at Atlanta Area Technical College. How can I paint you a picture of our life? We were faithful to the service of the Lord, and served him with all of our hearts. We trained our children from an early age to love God and to serve him daily. I guess you could say we were raising two preacher's kids.

I've often sat and thought about it and asked myself would I do it all over again? I cannot answer that question right now. As a child I always envisioned marriage as this great utopia of happiness and bliss, but I never dreamed in a million years that I was about to embark upon a journey which would alter how I processed success, happiness, loyalty, and love.

We had just purchased our first home in Lithonia, Georgia. My wife had just gotten a new good paying job and along with our two small children and two new vehicles, in our eyes everything was going well. We were happy, in love, and well on our way to becoming a dedicated husband and wife. Looking back in retrospect, we were ok. You know, I've always been a man who was and is very proud to be a father to my children and a husband to beautiful wife. I never thought that all of that would be tried, tested, and proven. Here I was, a young man trying to hold on to his words. Did I not stand before the altar at the Oak Grover Freewill Baptist Church, in Durham NC, that day and promised before God and man that I would love my wife, through sickness and in health, for richer or poor, forsaking all others, and vowing to stay with this woman until death parted us? Wow, isn't it amazing that while standing there and making those promises, you may not for one minute think about what you just said. There were some days I questioned my own sanity in why I said that.

The day was proceeding great, and I had settled into that just right position on the couch. I was holding a can of ice chilled coca cola and the remote controls to the TV when I heard this horrible cry for help. Startled and numb with anticipation of what awaited me just around the corner, I jumped up from the couch, and ran to the front room to see me my wife writhing with pain on the floor. She had just severely injured her back. Confused, I was at a loss for words as I stood there helplessly, praying silently. I guess you could say a flood of emotions ran over me that day. My wife was in severe pain and I could do nothing to help her.

I knew immediately that day that our lives would be altered forever. Isn't, it truly amazing how your whole life can change in sixty seconds? This was the beginning of the first year of a nine trail and wilderness experience. I can actually admit this now, but I was angry about our circumstances, and wondered why God would allow this to happen to us. I had been in the church all my life. I was the church musician at five years old. I could see God's hand upon me early in my life. Here I was the head of the household, and I didn't have a clue as to how I was going to handle the monumental tasks ahead of me. This was going to be a scary time. I know you've heard of people talk about going through a storm, well just imagine one of the storms lasting for a total of nine years. Yes, we were in this for nine years. I was being tried and pressed on every side. My life was not my own.

During that very first year of testing, I really felt hopeless and not prepared to take on what was coming down the road for us. It was like seeing the storm clouds gathering off in the distance and thinking, somebody is going to get some good rain after a while. It was as if I knew what the signs were, but did not grasp the full weight of what was going on in our lives. As I think about it now, I can't even tell you of the number of times I quit, but found myself rising early every morning, getting the kids ready for school and taking care of the needs of my wife. I remember fondly braiding my daughter's hair for school, not knowing what a mess I had created. My daughter never complained, because she knew it was from my heart. She probably changed it after she got to school anyway.

Because of my wife's back injury, she was bed ridden for days upon days. I never dreamed that faithfulness in marriage would include picking your wife up and carrying her to the restroom and then back to bed. I remember purchasing a twin sized bed for her, so that she would not have to climb stairs to go to her bedroom. All I knew was that I saw myself lying there on that bed, and knowing that she'd do the very same thing for me if the situation had been reversed. One never knows how deeply love can grow until you have a trial like this for nine years.

One thing I knew how to do was put on a good fake smile at church each Sunday. No one knew that we did not have food in the house and nothing but a pitcher of water in the refrigerator. I can't tell you the number of times God stretched a chicken that fed my whole family. But, by the grace of God, my kids never went to bed hungry. Yes, there were sacrifices made by me to keep my family together. Remember earlier I mentioned that we had just moved into our new home, had purchased two cars, and had a hefty mortgage to pay monthly. I did everything in my power to make money to help out. I can remember having five jobs at one time. Whew....I would not wish that upon my worst enemy.

Through it all, there was one thing I can thank God for and that was for my mama who taught me how to work and be a man. I am the youngest of ten siblings. My paternal mother died when I was just three years old, so my siblings and I were split up among five aunts and uncles. Since I was so young, the only person I knew as my mom was my aunt Gladys T. Ruth. She actually raised me. Man, she was a strict disciplinarian. All throughout my preschool, adolescent, and teen years, I thought the she was the meanest person alive. But as I look back over my life, I eventually realized that I was strategically placed in her home. She became my guardian of life; she taught me what it meant to be a real man. Without a father who to emulate, she taught me that hard work and integrity would be the tools that I would use to get me through what I was about to go through.

I know many of us have heard the phrase, going through a storm, well, I can personally testify that God will not only lead you through the storms of life, but guide the ship that has lost its way in the midst of the storm. Now I know lost is a strong word, but that is exactly where I was for many years. I guess one could say that we had gotten so comfortable with storms we started to consider them as normal.

This was not how I envisioned my life would be. There were times I wanted to just give up. There were many days I wanted to just get in the car and drive anywhere. Can I tell you something, during those times of despair, God would always send someone to give me a word of hope. They didn't know it, but they were words of encouragement and faith builders. Some of you may ask, "Pastor Ronnie, how did you do it?" How did you keep your sanity, what was it really like? I came home from work every day wishing I could take upon myself all of the pain and agony my wife endured daily. I even prayed to God that he would let me carry her burden just for one day. If I could have carried this cross for her, I would have gladly taken the load for her. But, unfortunately, I could do nothing but watch her lay there day in and day out. I did everything in my power every day to make her comfortable. Although I was working myself towards a slow impending heart attack, God gave me just enough strength for the next day. God gave me my bread daily. I was living day by day by faith, trusting God that any day now, the tide would break, the storm would pass, and everything would be normal again, but it never did until a total of nine years had passed.

There is no way I can physically tell you or write down all of the miracles God performed each day for me and my family. I can only do my best to describe a few of the circumstances and situations that I went through. To be honest with you, there were those times I thought God was paying me back for some wrong I had done or said. You know when you don't know the reason why something is happening to you, you start grasping for straws looking for something that makes sense.

In my dealings with others, I always tried to do the godly thing, dotting I's and crossing T's. I was thinking I must have done something that God was not pleased with. I would go on fasts for clarity of spirit, for God to reveal to me what was going on. Guess what? I never received a word back. Then I began to think that maybe, I hadn't done anything at all but perhaps this was somehow a test of some sort. Well, if this was a test, I was failing with flying colors, because, I didn't feel good about my situation. Wasn't I supposed to be joyful, and in all things giving thanks, because this was the will of God concerning me? Was I not to know that all things were working together for my good? Well, from my viewpoint, nothing was pulling together for me. Yes, I was confused, frustrated, and indifferent to my circumstances. I was somewhat irritated, not only about our financial plight, but I was aggravated that God would allow this to occur. It was as if Job 1 was being played out in the natural. Actually, I believed God was bragging on us, "Hey adversary, where are you going? What have you been doing? Oh, to and fro throughout the earth seeking whom I can devour." I can imagine God saying, "Consider Ronnie and Marsha." Listen, it's a powerful thing when God mentions your name for a test. We learned quickly that the storms you go through, and the testimony derived on the other side is not just for you and yours.

All too often we forget that there is no testimony unless there is a test. And we all know that a test is not given just for you to give back a memorized answer, but a test determines what you have learned throughout the experience. You see it's the experience that's more important, not just the right answer. You can always give the right answer and still have not learned why that answer is correct. It's the experience and the built relationship that God wants to reveal through the trial or temptation. Of course it's easy to talk about the hard times you had, but it's more important to have developed a lasting relationship with God through that trial.

What I learned through the experience was a developed relationship with God. I came to a point in my life that I had to let go of my ego, and totally rely on God. This was not an easy thing do because for a man, it's hard to tell another man about what's going on in your life. You see, as men we are so private. We don't easily admit to anyone that we are inadequate in any area of our life. I had to realize that no matter how well I could analyze a particular situation, I still needed someone else to help me. This actually saved my life. When you are drowning in water that is over your head, you don't care who throws you a life line.

My mama taught me something about water in rivers or lakes. She would always say "it doesn't matter whether or not you think you can swim, if you are drowning you need help because you cannot drink all of that water". I smile when I think about how much my mother sowed into my life. As I often think about what she was saying, it simply meant that no matter what you've acquired or obtained in life, everybody will need someone else to help them get through some difficult times in their life. I learned some great lessons about life during this period of my life. I believe that one of the greatest lessons I learned was that every man needs to feel wanted and appreciated. I loved the fact that I was the provider for my family in any circumstance or scenario. However, deep down inside of my soul, I lived each day in fear that if I didn't make it to my jobs, we would lose everything. I was afraid of failure and what people outside of our household would think. I finally had to admit that without God, I was not going to survive this ordeal. On the outside, I appeared to have it going on and under control, but inwardly, I was suffering from the reality of not letting go. I thought that if I kept it together long enough, everything would surely work out. This was my mistake. I was relying on my own abilities, and not God.

There is one thing I took away from my experience and that was the fact that while going through a storm, you do get stronger every day.

"Yet Will I Trust Him"

By Cindy Sumter

It was March 2012, and it was such a beautiful Saturday. Basketball playoffs had come around for the season, and my son had a game. I saw so many parents and kids I knew at the game site. The energy was high and joyful. I had watched 4 hours of basketball. My son played a good game and his school won. As I was leaving, I was stopped in my tracks by a pain that was so excruciating that I could not walk. The people around me could see the pain in my face. I could not move; all I could do was lean against the wall. A friend came and took me to the hospital.

The doctors in the emergency room took x-rays but they didn't find anything. However, I was still in pain not being able to sit, crouch or lay in any position. I had been given all kinds of medicine to relieve the pain, but nothing worked. They could not find the true source of the pain, so the doctor gave me a prescription for medication and suggested that I see an orthopedic doctor.

I finally located an orthopedic doctor and I was given more x-rays. Again, they saw nothing! The doctor was as truthful with me as he could be. "Ms. Sumter, I feel the pain is coming from your joints and you seem to be suffering with "Bursitis of the hip" so he prescribed therapy and ice packs. Receiving therapy twice a week, I began to feel better, but as the weather changed I felt the effects. As time went on, I needed a cane to walk. The pain began to last for days. My doctor realized that I was getting worse and scheduled me for more tests.

After fighting with insurance companies for an MRI (magnetic resonance imaging), I was finally given the authorization to go forward with testing. While taking the MRI, the technicians found something and got further authorization from the insurance company to get a contrast (a 3D image using color).

This was the beginning of my journey. Three days after the MRI, my orthopedic doctor discussed with me the test reading. It showed a huge mass, bigger than he had ever seen. His eyes filled with tears as he apologized for having misdiagnosed my condition. He referred me to his best friend from college who is an Orthopedic Oncologist Surgeon. An appointment was scheduled with this doctor at Emory who is considered the top doctor (Best) in the country. When I arrived for my appointment, he showed me the mass on the MRI disk and said he needed to do a biopsy to determine his next step.

Surprisingly, I was asked to sit on the table to begin the biopsy. I thought I was just coming in to meet him! The doctor said, " I don't want you to be alarmed, but the mass is enormous and I must find out if it is malignant or benign." Once the biopsy was completed, he told me he would call me regarding the results. Dr. Monson explained that the tumor was growing and tearing through my muscles, tissues, and ligaments. He looked at me and said I really don't know how you have endured living with this pain this length of time.

A week had gone by and I hadn't heard from the doctor's office. I was told by his secretary that Dr. Monson was in a three-day conference regarding my case. He was setting up a top team of doctors to best serve me and he would contact me.

I went into my prayer closet and began to pray, asked God for healing. I reminded Him that no weapon formed against me shall prosper (Isaiah 54:17). I told Him I trusted and believed in His word. I affirmed I will not be fearful because he hadn't given me a spirit of fear, but a sound mind. I began to wail saying by your stripes I am healed, over and over! I requested instant healing as my soul became quiet and meditative. It was later that I heard a small quiet voice say, "you will be healed but you will go through a process." I began to cry out and thank Him for sending me a word. I didn't understand it but I did know I would be healed.

When my phone rang Friday morning at 8 a.m., as my feet hit the floor, I knew in my spirit it was the doctor with a report that my biopsy results were malignant. He told me that I have cancer called Synovial Sarcoma. My next response was, okay what are we going to do about it? He reaffirmed that he had been in conference on my case and had chosen his team. He wanted me to meet Dr. Rizzo, Dr. Read and later Dr. Goodette.

It is now Sunday morning, I couldn't wait to get up and get dressed for church. It is something about being in the assembly of the house of God. During service Bishop Johnathan Alvarado sensed something, the spirit was high and the whole congregation was crying out. He called for a healing line and began to call out different ailments of afflictions in the body. He called out Cancer and I got up along with others and went to the line. They anointed my head with oil and laid hands on me and began to pray for my healing. After service Bishop and Co-Pastor let me know they were in this fight with me. I just love them and I am thankful to my church family for the love they showed me throughout this cancer journey.

When I met with Dr. Rizzo, she explained that the lymph node from my groin area would be removed and that she would and place a dual port in my chest. She explained why the dual port was necessary and it was the only way the chemo medicine could get into my body to attack that cancer. I was scheduled for several more tests to determine if my heart was strong enough to endure the harsh chemotherapy.

Next I met Dr. Read, Radiation Oncologist. My test results were back and my heart was strong enough.

Surgery was scheduled with Dr. Rizzo. Dr. Read explained that although the team sees this type of cancer all the time, my case was unique. They have case studies for fifteen to thirty years of age for this type of cancer; however, there is not a study for my age group or the size of the tumor. At this time I was 52 years young and determined to live!

I notified my supervisor at work that I needed to take time off because of the planned procedure. I didn't want to go into details yet, but Jane, the accountant figured it out; she was a newly breast cancer survivor. She was my angel sent from God and she was so helpful to me during this time. I was still trying to embrace the diagnosis of cancer myself and everything was happening so fast.

The surgery to place a dual port in my chest and to remove a lymph node from my groin went well. The following week I spoke with Dr. Monson and he informed me that the lymph node was negative, meaning cancer had not spread to any other area. He also informed me that I would be out of work starting immediately and I would be out indefinitely. He warned me that the treatment will be harsh chemotherapy for four to six rounds, (4 to 6 months of chemo) then laser radiation and then surgery. Dr. Monson broke down harsh chemotherapy to me, meaning I would be in the hospital five days hooked up to the medication twenty-four hours a day all five days. Then released for home and the next day I would begin to receive shots for ten days to build up my immune system from the chemotherapy. This actually meant every twenty one days I would be in the hospital. Wow this was a lot I was hearing. As I would receive new information daily regarding my new diagnosis of cancer, all I could do was trust God and know he would work everything out for my good. I also knew I had to remain positive no matter what kind of report I would receive. I was going to believe in the report of the Lord.

The supervisors (Andrea, Willa, Rick and Vincent) and team members on the job were very sympathetic and were eager to help however they could. My last day at work was long and exhausting. I was thankful for the love and compassion everyone on the job showed me before I left the GICC facility.

Before I left for hospital I kissed my son off to school and prayed with him. He didn't want to go but it was 9th grade final exams, he had to go. I know he was scared but I tried to reassure him everything would be okay. With Bible in hand, luggage and iPad I left for the hospital not knowing what to really expect, but I had joy and peace. During the ride to Emory Hospital with Tyrone, a friend, my girlfriend Kathy called and we prayed that everything would be successful.

I arrived at the hospital and was greeted on the 7th floor by nurses at the front desk who wheeled me down to my room. God had given me peace that surpassed all understanding as I got connected to the chemo. Everyone was surprised that I wasn't having any side of effects of nausea, vomiting and dry mouth.

I noticed my faith was growing more and more each day. As different people came in and out of my room, I was witnessing. They spoke of the peacefulness that radiated in my room. It was now time to go home and although I was weak, with no appetite, I was happy to be going home.

At Winship Cancer Center where I was taken to get shots that helped build up my immune system I sat next to someone who was scared of the whole cancer journey. I found myself witnessing to this young lady of about twenty years old. For the next nine days as I got my shots, I noticed people were there of all races, male and female, young and old. Some were getting chemotherapy for two to three hours a day; some were waiting to receive radiation for whatever reason. As for me, I was just sitting there waiting to get my shots and witnessing about the goodness of Jesus. I realized this was just a process until healing was manifested.

After round one of chemotherapy, I was told my hair would begin to fall out. At this point my hair was longer than shoulder length. I went and got a sassy hair cut so it wouldn't be so dramatic when it would begin to fall out. You know, I was determined not to give Satan any chances to start bothering me about hair. So as my hair began to fall out just before cycle two, I was ready for it mentally.

Well, twenty-one days were up. It was time to return to the hospital for round two of chemo and five more days in the hospital. While in the hospital, I knew what to expect this time. My hair was still falling out. I would wake up with patches of hair on the pillow. I had no appetite and didn't want any hospital food. I was so thankful for my church family for all of their visits.

I was in my room waiting to be released to go home from the hospital. On the next day I started my shots again to build up immune system from chemo. On the eighth day of my shots, my back began to ache so I couldn't continue taking shots. Now I'm bald, clean and shiny head. Everyone kept asking if I was getting a wig. I said no! I would put on lipstick, eye shadow and big earrings and out I would go, bald and courageous. Many people at the cancer center said they were encouraged by my self-confidence. By now, all of body hair was gone.

Two cycles of harsh chemo had been completed. Next they wanted to check and see if the tumor had shrunk. The doctors were not expecting it to have shrunk, but I reminded them I wasn't like most of their patients. I proclaimed it with great confidence that, "I am a child of the King, and I know it has shrunk!" I went to take more tests, and to my doctors' surprise the cancerous tumor had shrunk. I knew God was going to do it because of my trust and faith in him.

The hardest part of the journey was explaining my condition to my son. He was in denial that I had cancer. He said I had a tumor and it was being treated with chemotherapy. My son's grandfather (my dad) passed from prostate cancer, and my son watched him endure it because he lived with us. My son also has an issue with hospitals because his grandmother (my mom) went to the hospital and never came back home. All I could do was reassure him I would come back home from the hospital each time. Philippians 4:13 is my son's favorite scripture. I reminded him of this, that "I can do all things through Christ who strengthens me."

July and August brought even harsher chemotherapy. The last session in August was the hardest, round four. My nurses and technicians laughed and said sarcastically, "We finally got a cancer patient!" because in the beginning I never experienced the sickness that comes with chemo. This had been my weakest point; couldn't eat, no taste buds, nauseated, throwing up, dry mouth, etc., you name it I was doing it. My body came home weaker than ever. I was dizzy and needed assistance from the car to the house and up the stairs to my bed. I awaken the next day for my shots very weak and still dizzy. This time I could only take shots for five days. Sharp shooting pains began to ache in my lower back. All I could do was cry out to God in the midst of it all, I had no doubt that He was with me. My doctor felt that my body needed a break so the shots were stopped. I was free of appointments for 2 weeks.

I had another evaluation in August to see if the tumor had shrunk anymore. It was exactly like my God had said; once again it had shrunk. Both doctors were amazed again and said," you keep talking to your Daddy (meaning God) because he is definitely doing what you are asking". Then Dr. Read and Dr. Monson were at odds. One doctor wanted another round of chemo and the other doctor wanted to start laser radiation. I begin to pray to my God (daddy) and ask him please lead and guide them to what is best for me.

Another school year had started and my son was in 10th grade and attending a new school. I didn't want him to keep experiencing me being away. He didn't maintain his grade point average in 9th grade, so he had to go back to the school in his home district. I was thankful he had gotten promoted to 10th grade because he had a lot on his plate worrying if his mom would live or die.

My desire was not to do chemo again but I wanted God's will to be done. Dr. Read got his wish and I started Laser Radiation. I was so happy and thankful to my Lord and Savior! I thought of the song by Roberta Martin, He Knows Just How Much We Can Bear. God knew my body couldn't take another round of harsh chemo, and my son needed to see me daily to assist with his academics/ mental/school activities.

Now it was time to meet and be checked by a new doctor named Dr. Goodette. I was scheduled for twenty-five applications of laser radiations Monday through Friday only. I would go and receive treatment which was to me so much easier than chemotherapy, but I never complained. The best part was I didn't have to be away from my son. My appointments were during the day while my son was in school, so this was great.

The laser radiation application procedures went from August to part of October. It was now the first week of October and I was on my count down of five applications to go. I saw the doctor every Tuesday. She checked my skin and found a blister that had developed on my right hip and butt. I was given a prescription to heal it. As time went on the blister wasn't healing, but my faith was in God. He had been my source thus far and I was determined to continue trusting him for the healing of the blister.

On the last day of laser radiation, I arrived to my appointment late. I walked in the waiting area and people began to give me their phone numbers. I was curious as to what was occurring; they had heard it was my last day. They hugged me and thanked me for being so supportive and encouraging to all of them during such a difficult time. I was overwhelmed and thankful, but most of all, humbled.

When I got to the back for my final radiation treatment, all the technicians, nurses and doctors presented me with a certificate with their signatures and quotes. Many were saying how positive and how easy I was to treat. They also had phone numbers for me to stay in contact with them. I was so moved. I told them it was God that had kept me. I thanked all of them for their special kindness and dedication in caring for me. As I was leaving I began to praise God as I walked to the car. It made me say you never know who is watching you as you are being tested, so always let them see God, no matter what you may be feeling or going through mentally and physically. My God is an awesome God and he takes care of his children! My Bishop Johnathan Alvarado and Co-Pastor Dr. Toni Alvarado, ministerial staff and all cancer survivors laid their hands on my afflicted body Sunday, October 27th before I went into surgery the next day.

I arrived at the hospital at 6:30 a.m. My surgery was successful. Everyone I passed I would proclaim "I'm cancer free, cancer free." As I arrived on the third floor, all the nurses said I was mighty alert for someone who just had surgery. "I'm cancer free, and I want to shout it from the mountain top. God said I would go through a process, but I would be healed. Today I am healed.

My surgery consisted of removing a large sixteen cm tumor from the muscular area of my hip and butt. Once the tumor was cut out and lifted up, my bone had begun to deteriorate. My doctor shaved the bone until he didn't see any more deterioration. I was cut from my lower back down to below my hip on the right side. Over 200 stitches were used inside and out to close the wound. I now have a permanent limp. But just know if I had to choose between life and a limp, I'm sure you know the answer.

The same day as surgery, a physical therapist came to my room. She asked if I could move to the edge of the bed. I made it to the edge of bed and sat. She placed the walker in front of me and said see if you can stand. I grabbed that walker and stood and walked out of my room to the hallway and back to my bed. She looked at me strange and asked when did you have surgery? I replied earlier today, and she said there was no way I should be able to do any of this, and definitely not walking like this. I said my God is still in the miracle working business. I began to give Him praise and shouted hallelujah and waved my hands giving Him all the praise, glory and honor. No one else can do me like Jesus. Elder Jeff walked in my room said Bishop has been praying to see a miracle. I will call him and let him know all about this miracle. We are so excited because the plan the doctors had for me was to go to rehab from the hospital to learn how to stand and put weight on the hip and learn how to walk, but God had another plan. When you trust in the

Lord and don't lean to your own understanding, but acknowledge Him in all of his ways, and I promise you He will give you a blessing.

Everyone came by my room telling me I was the talk of the hospital. No one could believe I was walking. A new therapist came and said she didn't believe the talk, so I had to show her. I moved to the edge of the bed, grabbed my walker and walked out of the room to the hallway. I told her that the therapist from the previous day had said I could try the stairs, and she said no, that I was not yet ready for the stairs. I asked her where the stairs were, and she indicated they were through the doors next to me. I asked her if I could try so she opened the door. I walked through the door and to the step. I counted ten steps. I pushed the walker aside, grabbed the handrails and walked up the ten steps to her amazement. She explained to me to step with my left leg and lift the right leg since I had surgery on the right side. I took a breather at the top of the steps because going down was different; down ten steps and to my room. The next day, I walked around the entire floor. Half way around I gave a wave of praise to God for His healing power. I walked, stepped, and praised God some more. The therapist asked, "Now what?" my reply was, "I'm going home tomorrow!" She said you think so and I said yes, God just told me. I have surrendered my all to Him and I can't thank Him enough. What a Mighty God I serve. He just keep doing great thing for me over and over again.

On Thursday morning, I was given the clearance to go home. Hooray! I was so excited that I'm calling friends to come pick me up. It is hard to believe that earlier on in this process, my doctors had said I had a 1 in 5 million chance of living. My favorite scripture through this entire journey was "Though he slay me, yet will I trust in Him (Job 13:15)." I know God is my SOURCE and everything or everyone He may use in the process is the resource He is using at the time. I can tell you without a shadow of a doubt there is nothing too hard for God. I am a living testimony of His goodness and His healing power. I know I couldn't make it on my own. I trust and believe in Him. Every step of this journey has been a faith walk.

Once I was release from the hospital, I was home for 4 months. During this time I was going back and forth to doctor appointments, making sure my wound was healing correctly, and of course getting all those stitches removed because none were dissolvable. I learned how to walk better with a walker and cane. I also had to take MRI and CT scans of the hip and buttock area every 3 months. God has constantly renewed my strength as times were lonely and hard. I learned how to totally rely and lean on God for everything.

My doctor finally gave me the okay for rehab for the hip area in March 2014. I started out going to rehab twice a week and it was killing me. I hadn't been able to exercise for a year. All of my muscles were tight. I couldn't do simple things like crossing my legs. My therapist suggested water aerobics therapy for the next couple of months to try and loosen me up better. I could do so many more things in the water than I could do in regular rehab on mats and machines. My endurance and stamina was increasing also.

I had been out of work for a year in May 2014 when I received a certified letter from my job, explaining it was a hardship in my department without me and not knowing when I would return, they had decided to open my position for new hire. They asked me not to worry because I was still employed with the same salary. You know I went into my prayer closet before I called the job. Please tell me who wouldn't serve a GOD like this. I gave the Executive Director a call. She asked me to please get well soon and that they would see me when I got back. This was nothing but God continuing to reassure me that He is in control of everything.

If you are wondering how I am making it being off work so long, it was God and I have always been a tither. God has been my source and short/long term disability has been my resource. These resources are much smaller than my normal income when working. Not one time have I been in need of anything and I have continued to pay my tithes/offering/pastoral care and any special times of giving at my church. No mortgage, utility, car insurance, credit card bill, grocery, etc. has been missed or late. There has been no lack in my house. All fees for sports at school, lunch money, clothing, etc. for my son continue to be available.

It is now October 2014 and I have been cancer free for one year. I am now getting some possible dates on when I may be able to return to work. They are tossing the dates of December 2014 or January 2015. Through this process I have been taught how to wait on God. My faith has grown so much and I really know God for myself. Just know God has been my strength, my rock and my shield during this time of recovery.

EPILOGUE
THROUGH IT ALL:
Wisdom of the Ages

This inspiring book by a group of seniors at Grace Church International is filled with life experiences that can be wisdom to us all. These individuals chose to share insights about their lives, in an effort to instill hope, the ability to overcome, and the agony and pain of survival. *Through It All: Wisdom of the Ages* captures the lives of few but takes us through time as we witness the grace and hand of God in the lives of His people.

When you read the book of Exodus there were stone memorials, places named that identified the struggle and victory of God's people as they journeyed towards the land of promise. In the 17th chapter, when the people were thirsty and complained against Moses, God instructed him to take his rod and strike at Horeb. When water came flowing out of the rock and the people drank he called the place Massah and Meribah because of the contention of the children of Israel and because they tempted the Lord. Later in this same chapter as God's people were fighting against the Amalekites and defeated them, an altar was built named, "The Lord Is My Banner".

So, we see these biblical stories that open our eyes to people struggling in their journey, yet overcoming. These contemporary stories permit us to connect with issues of rejection, neglect, substance abuse, personal injury, deceit. But through it all, we are able to gain the wisdom of character, trust, forgiveness, starting over and victory.

LaVoris L. Holloway

Pastor, Grace Church International at Clayton

Rex, GA

Author Bio's

 Vivian McClain is the Director of Property Management for Generation Mortgage Co. Vivian has four children and three grandsons and she is praying for a granddaughter. She is actively involved in the Seasoned with Grace Senior Ministry at Grace Church International.

 Mary Moore serves as ministry leader for Christian Discipleship and G.R.O.W. Women Ministry at Grace Church International at Clayton. She is the co-director of Seasoned with Grace Senior Ministry. Mary has been married to Bobby for forty-four years; they are parents of two children and four grandchildren.

 Connie Thomas and her spouse Lawrence serve as Deacons at Grace Church International at Clayton. Connie is also a member of the Evangelism Team, Women's Ministry Council, Intercessory Team, and she volunteers as the church office assistant. She and Lawrence will celebrate forty-seven years together in January 2015. They are parents of six children, twenty-five grandchildren, and ten great grandchildren.

Mae Alice Reggy, Ph.D. is an educator and author. She has done mission work in more than fifty countries around the world. Presently she lives in Atlanta, Georgia where she serves on the Adjunct Faculty at Beulah Heights University and on the ministerial team at Grace Church International.

 Gregory Y. Goode is an ordained minister and has served as a missionary in Ghana and other parts of the world. He is a husband of twenty-nine years and a father of three. Gregory serves on the ministerial team at Grace Church International.

 Selin Rives is a member of Grace Church International where she is an active member of the Seasoned with Grace Senior Ministry, the Pastoral Care Ministry and the Worship and Arts Ministry. She is currently employed at a family and children's treatment center as a mental health professional. Selin has two sons and three grandchildren.

 Cindy Sumter is an Event Manager at the Georgia International Convention Center in College Park, Georgia. Cindy is a prayer warrior and is involved in the Seasoned with Grace Senior and Pastoral Care Ministries at Grace Church International. She is the mother of one son.

K. Nature Mosley King is a member and employee (receptionist) of Grace Church International Headquarters. She serves as Director of Grace Church International Seasoned with Grace Senior Ministry as well as Pastoral Care Chief of Staff. Nature is married to Ronald and their blended family consists of seven children and fifteen grandchildren.

 Jeffrey Lewis is Lead Elder of Grace Church International Headquarters. Jeff serves on the GCI ministerial team as well as the Seasoned with Grace Senior Ministry and the Director of Pastoral Care and Sacraments. He is employed at Shepard Center in Atlanta, Georgia. Jeff is married to Charmaine and has four children.

 Margaret Griffin Baker is a retired Registered Nurse. She is the mother of four daughters and grandmother of eight. Margaret is an active member of Grace Church International.

 Jesse Wright is an employee of Grace Church International Headquarters. Jesse has two daughters and six grandchildren all residing in Chattanooga, Tennessee.

Eunice L. Thomas-Heath is a New York Apple now a Georgia Peach. She is employed by Gregory B. Levitt and Sons Funeral Homes. Eunice is a member of the Red Hatters Society and she enjoys being a Mary Kay Beauty Consultant. She is a servant of the Lord at Grace Church International where she serves on the Seasoned with Grace Senior Ministry, Prayer, New Members Orientation Ministries, Pastoral Care, and Altar Workers Ministries.

 Bobby Moore was born in Greenville, Mississippi. He retired from General Dynamic L. S. in Troy, Michigan. He serves as an usher and member of the Men's Ministry at Grace Church International at Clayton. He is married to Mary A. Webb; they are parents of two children and four grandchildren. His degrees include an Associate of Applied Science (AAS) in Electronics and a Bachelor of Arts in Business Administration from Siena Heights University in Adrian, Michigan.

 Edna Wise is married with two children. She serves as an usher and is a Pastoral Care team member at Grace Church International. Edna also serves with the Seasoned with Grace Senior Ministry.

Vanessa Mitchell Goode is a native of Gallatin, Tennessee. She received her degrees in Elementary Education and Special Education from Tennessee State University in Nashville, Tennessee. She is the wife of Gregory Goode, and the mother of three, Gregory, II, Allyson, and Lydia. Mrs. Goode is a retired educator of thirty-two years and continues to volunteer in her community schools. She is presently working with the Seasoned with Grace Senior Ministry and Pastoral Care at Grace Church International.

 Robert Williams was born and raised in New Jersey and Connecticut. He later moved to Georgia. He and his wife, Jeanette, have two daughters and one son. Robert received an Associate Degree in Applied Science and Electronic Technology from DeVry University. He presently works for AT&T. Robert is an ordained deacon and serves as an usher and member of the Seasoned with Grace Senior Ministry.

 Zelda Lucas has been a member of Grace Church International since 1996 and has been an employee there for fourteen years. The Ministry areas she serves in are Diaconal, Worship and Arts, Seasoned with Grace, and Pastoral Care. She has been married to Scotty Lucas for thirty-five years. They have three sons, two daughters-in-law, and four grandchildren.

Cheryl Moon has been married for forty-five years with three sons and six grandchildren. She worked in the social services industry for ten years. Cheryl has been a member of Grace Church International for twenty years. Throughout the years she has served in several ministries such as the Senior Ministry and Missions and the Street Team just to name a few. She is currently serving as Christian Care Director in the Women Ministry Leadership Council. She graduated from DeKalb County Leadership Institute and is continuing her education in Sociology.

 Ronnie Thompson is a native of Lumberton, North Carolina. He is the youngest son amongst ten children and was raised by a God-fearing aunt. He is currently an ordained Elder at Grace Church International where he has served for twenty years. Ronnie received his undergraduate degree from North Carolina Central University (1980) and his Masters of Divinity from Luther Rice Seminary (2012). A godly husband for thirty-four years, proud father, man of wisdom, the Word, and strength, Ronnie knows what it means to be a survivor.

Be encouraged
Blessings
Margaret Baker

Gods Grace &
Faith Dutton Blessings

Carmen, for your support.
Thanks for your support.
Be Blessed & Enjoy.
nature

Wisdom not shared is wisdom
Lost forever Jessica Light

Be blessed!

Angys & Arrd
&
Vanessa Yoods

Made in the USA
Lexington, KY
18 April 2016